The Book of (Even More) Awesome

"The guru of small joys."
—*Toronto Star*

"Neil Pasricha makes ordinary days light up with awesomeness."
—Gretchen Rubin, #1 *New York Times* bestselling author of *The Happiness Project*

"What comes after awesome? There's only one thing that can surpass such an idea . . . and that idea is *even more awesome.* Read this book to go above and beyond your most awesome day."
—Chris Guillebeau, *New York Times* bestselling author of *The $100 Startup*

"Ranging from laugh-out-loud funny to poignant (but not fluffy), Pasricha's compilation feels close to universally applicable. . . . Pasricha doesn't mandate a way to live well. In many simple ways, he just reminds us we already do."
—*The Huffington Post*

"What Jerry Seinfeld was to stand-up, Neil Pasricha is to blogging."
—*The Globe and Mail* (Toronto)

The Book of Awesome

"Optimism for the rest of us. Sunny without being saccharine, it's a countdown of life's little joys that reads like a snappy Jerry Seinfeld monologue by way of Maria von Trapp."
—*The Vancouver Sun*

continued

"If Ernest Hemingway were alive today, he'd say 'I'm one hundred and twelve years old. Someone please kill me.' But I also think he'd like this book."

—Justin Halpern, #1 *New York Times* bestselling author of *Sh*t My Dad Says*

"Pasricha emerges a committed but inviting optimist, combating life's unending stream of bad news by identifying opportunities to share a universal high five with humanity."

—*Publishers Weekly*

"Honors the little joys of life."   —*USA Today*

"It's nice to remind yourself of life's sweeter side and the pleasures to be had from the small things—like peeling the thin plastic film off new electronic gadgets . . . and sneaking your own cheap snacks into the cinemas. . . . Life really is awesome after all."   —*The Guardian* (U.K.)

"The awesomest part about *The Book of Awesome* is the realization that if you enjoy the simple moments of awesome in your life, you will be happier."

—Ben Huh, *New York Times* bestselling author of *I Can Has Cheezburger?*

"*The Book of Awesome* gives me 14,001 things to be happy about. Bravo for taking note of the sunny side of life!"

—Barbara Ann Kipfer, author of *14,000 Things to Be Happy About*

"Even a cynical white person can't deny the appeal of *The Book of Awesome*."

—Christian Lander, *New York Times* bestselling author of *Stuff White People Like*

Titles by Neil Pasricha

The Book of Awesome

The Book of (Even More) Awesome

The Book of (Holiday) Awesome

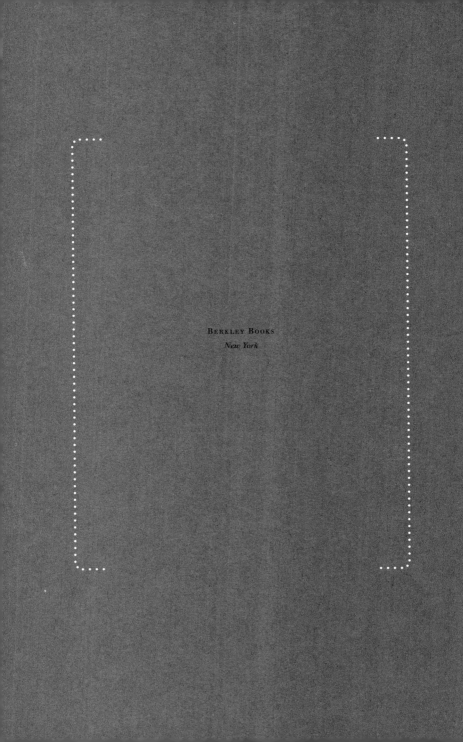

BERKLEY BOOKS
New York

The

Book

of

(Holiday)
Awesome

Neil Pasricha

THE BERKLEY PUBLISHING GROUP
Published by the Penguin Group
Penguin Group (USA) LLC
375 Hudson Street, New York, New York 10014, USA

USA • Canada • UK • Ireland • Australia • New Zealand • India • South Africa • China

penguin.com

A Penguin Random House Company

Berkley trade paperback ISBN: 978-0-425-25372-4

The Library of Congress has cataloged the Amy Einhorn / G. P. Putnam's Sons hardcover edition as follows:
Pasricha, Neil.
The book of (holiday) awesome / Neil Pasricha.
p.   cm.
ISBN 978-0-399-15859-9
1. Christmas—Humor.   2. Holidays—Humor.   I. Title.
PN6231.C36P37   2011   2011034271
818'.602—dc23

PUBLISHING HISTORY
Amy Einhorn / G. P. Putnam's Sons hardcover edition / November 2011
Berkley trade paperback edition / November 2013

PRINTED IN THE UNITED STATES OF AMERICA

10   9   8   7   6   5   4   3   2   1

Cover design by gray318.

All photos from iStock (istockphoto.com) with the exception of "When the wrapping paper lines up perfectly" by Leslie
Richardson, "When the Christmas tree gives the only light in the room" by Ben Crossley, "When you can actually hear it
snowing" by Sam Javanrouh, "When your gelt melts perfectly in your mouth instead of in the wrapper" by Liz West, and
"Intense post-Halloween candy trades" by Thane Plambeck. Thanks to all of them for their beautiful images.

Fa-la-la-la-la-la-la-la-AWESOME!

So what's this all about?

....

Holidays are stressful.

Long shopping lists, **tricky travel**, and visiting in-laws all snowball into busy weeks of blood-boiling bliss. When that tree's wedged up high, when the presents are all wrapped, when the party dress is squeezed on . . . well, sometimes you just want eggnog and a nap.

And that's when I hope you'll flip open **The Book of (Holiday) Awesome** for a little escape between gravy boats and Christmas lights, between holiday baking and board game nights. Flip it open when you're tired, flip it open when you're mad, **flip it open to feel festive**, flip it open to feel glad.

Because holidays give us great breaks and holidays give us great times. They're full of family moments and little chances to unwind. From the big banging moments at the end of the year to the little ones in the spring and the fall, it's fun bouncing through them with loved ones, and fun bouncing through them at all. Sometimes between **Christmas card stresses** and dinnertime messes, it's easy to forget we're celebrating some pretty big things: the birth of a country, **a time to remember**, a day to give thanks, or a Monday off in September.

So let your brain drift back to good memories, let your

mind enjoy old times, **let your body slip into the awesome**, and let yourself relax and unwind.

I hope you have a very awesome holiday.

Love,

Neil

Getting a Christmas card from someone you thought you lost touch with

. . . .

Surprise!

Your friendship is alive.

When the clock starts ticking and you **scatter and splatter** in distant directions, sometimes it seems like life's bumps and deflections sever ties and cut you off from the world.

Maybe kids arrived and you moved away, **maybe college came and you left for the day**, maybe your job got changed or you argued and fought, maybe time just rolled on and you stayed in the same spot.

But somehow that thick black line of friendship slowly faded and went away. Somehow the phone calls stopped coming as tomorrow became today.

And then! Out of nowhere! When you open a card and see the familiar cursive of an old friend . . . well, it's like a little light in your heart is finally flickering again.

Your eyes pop and jaw drops as you salivate and **soak up every word** of that little package of love. And between the lines of job updates and the words about the kids is an even bigger message hidden right below the lid.

It says: "I'd like to get together again. I remember our laughs and know how busy we've been. But I hope you agree that, **since life's short and always wavering**, it's even more important our friendship is worth enjoying . . . and worth savoring."

AWESOME!

Walking into a grocery store and seeing the first shipment of eggnog

··

My buddy Mike's a sugar rat.

Whenever I visit his apartment downtown we end up ordering pizza, **watching old movies**, and playing video games. And when we're done snacking I always turn to him and say, "Hey, man, you got any chocolate or anything?" We're close, me and Mike, and have long passed the point where we're too polite to only eat when we're offered food. I'll hunt around the man's fridge like it's my own and I expect him to do the same.

Now the funny thing is that when I ask him, Mike usually just heads to the kitchen and starts hunting through cupboards of really, really old Tupperware, **under stale half loaves of bread at the bottom of the freezer,** and behind dusty food processors above the fridge. Yes, he hunts until he pulls out a surprise pack of unopened Reese's Peanut Butter Cups or peels the lid off a brand-new tub of ice cream.

My buddy Mike's a sugar rat.

See, he doesn't trust himself to have the good stuff in view, so he hides it in the cracks and corners of his place and hopes he'll forget it. This is known as the **Out Of Sight, Out Of Mind Diet Plan**, and it seems to work wonders for him. After all, he doesn't gorge himself on candy bars that much, and whenever a sweet-toothed pal is jonesing for a fix, he just goes hunting until he finds the gold.

I think Mike's whole theory is the same one behind the entire eggnog industry.

Just think! They're saying, "Here, enjoy this deliciously sweet and creamy drink, but—ah ah ah! You can only have it in December. Here, grind some cinnamon on top, **spike it with rum**, break out the crystal punch glasses for a sugary surprise in your mouth, but—ah ah ah! There's none available in the new year."

And thank goodness, **thank gracious**, thank God for that.

Because if we drank eggnog all the time we'd get pretty fat.

AWESOME!

Plugging in your Christmas lights from last year and having them all work

....

Whether you swirl strings of lights around your front hedges, **line them up perfectly around the roof**, or use them as a glittery frame around your garage door, you know as well as I do that one dead bulb dims the whole scene.

That's why it's a beautiful moment when you peel open that musty cardboard box in the basement, untie that tightly wound ball of **glass-and-wire knots**, and plug them in for the great big show.

When the bulbs are all sparkling it's time to get the whole neighborhood shining in a shimmering little moment of

AWESOME!

When that kid crying in the mall isn't your kid

··

There's nothing like a good old-fashioned **holiday hissy fit** in an elbow-to-elbow packed mall to help soothe your fraying nerves.

Whether it's the snotty-nosed toddler wailing on Santa's lap, **the sweaty snowsuit screamer** on the floor of the toys section, or your everyday baby bawler yelling to the food court heavens, it doesn't matter.

It's just a migraine moment in the middle of mall mayhem.

And whether you're taking care of your baby brother, **babysitting the neighbors**, or wheeling around your own **mutant offspring**, we've all been there. We all know the stress, we see the staring eyes, we all know the pain, and . . . we do sympathize.

But it's still great when that kid crying in the mall just isn't your kid.

Hark! The herald angels sing.

Glory to the kid-free king.

AWESOME!

That moment near the holidays when there's suddenly cookies, chocolate, and candy everywhere

. . . .

Roll those rum balls, sprinkle sparkles on the shortbread, and dump the bulk bag of candy canes in the crystal dish by the secretary's desk.

If we're gonna get fat, let's get fat together.

AWESOME!

Getting the person you have a crush on for office Secret Santa

I work in an office.

Crystal bowls of red jelly beans, **snowman ties**, and festive cheer all spring up in the cubicle hallways as the holidays get near. And sure, sure, holidays are about big love, family time, and being at home, but it's fun getting in the mood with the folks we spend our days with too.

And nothing says **Christmas Is Coming** more than the classic **Secret Santa** moment at your workplace. We all drop our names into a bowl and everyone picks one out of the pot to buy them a little present within the five- or ten-dollar budget.

Getting the person you have a crush on for your office Secret Santa is a beautiful moment. When you unfold the paper and reveal the object of your desire, suddenly you've got an excuse to send a signal to someone you've been flirting with all year.

Yes, now's the time to ditch the movie gift certificates, **box of chocolates**, and stuffed animals in Christmas hats and send them a little bit of love. Of course, the big question is—how? Here are three tips for some festive love:

1. **Ban the briefs.** Sending sexy lingerie or a bottle of cologne packaged in a box with a sweaty six-pack on the cover is way overboard. Coming across as the Christmas Pervert will get you on the Naughty List.

2. **Be a spy.** What's their favorite coffee? Where do they eat lunch? What do they do on weekends? Talk to their friends, see what's on their desk, and try to give them something personal that shows you know them.

3. **Make it a pair.** A home run could be including time together as part of your present. Try a classy "Homemade Lunch" in the cafeteria where you bust out your Grandma's famous meatball recipe, or how about a set of coupons for "Five Free Coffee Runs," where they get to join you for donuts down the street.

Getting the person you have a crush on for your office Secret Santa is a great big moment of opportunity. Because let's be honest—a lot of great relationships start up at work, and there's nothing wrong with telling your special someone that they mean something to you.

Make your move.

AWESOME!

The first big snowfall
of the season

．．．

Crystal flakes form in space before floating down from
cloudy skies.

Soon blankets of white coat sidewalks like icing and **frosty
corners freeze** in shady yards by the shed. Scarves twist tightly
around necks, noses sniffle and turn red, and everyone walks
the streets with wide eyes and snowy lashes. Boots slip and
slide on the sidewalk, **mittens swipe seats in the park**, and
branches glow under a silent new moonlit world.

Sometimes the first snowfall gets your bones excited about
everything the season brings: family moments, **quiet times**, eating foods you loved as a kid. It's a sign of venturing into a new
world while bunkering into an old one at the same time.

When the snow flies down for the first time everything
slows down around you and **nostalgia bombs** burst in your
brain . . . of slip-sliding to school on sidewalks, slushy snowball fights in the park, and sticky mittens rolling snowmen
with your sisters on the front lawn . . .

AWESOME!

When the neighbor shovels your little patch of the sidewalk

. . . .

S idewalks bring us together.

Fences split yards, **lawns divide homes**, and invisible property lines are scribbled on dusty blueprints in city archives. But somehow those little strips of concrete tie us all together and connect the dots between our lives.

It's a beautiful moment when a friendly neighbor shovels the snow off of your walk after a winter snowstorm. Swaddled in snow-packed mitts, **sweaty scarves**, and salty boots, they're just lending a helping hand of kindness and some friendly season's greetings.

AWESOME!

When strangers wish you happy holidays

....

Holidays are hectic.

Gift shopping, **mall hopping**, money dropping, and through it all you're planning in-law sleepovers, giant family dinners, and complicated travel plans.

It's nice in these roaring revved-up moments when a complete stranger catches your eye and wishes you a heartfelt happy holidays.

Whether it's the cashier at the grocery store, the receptionist at your gym, or the lady getting a perm beside you at the salon, it's nice scoring that warm little season's greetings to remind us we're all chasing the same ol' thing.

That's right: Love, big hugs, **family time**, and cozy company right when we need it most.

AWESOME!

Eating all the chocolates in your Advent calendar at once

....

Nice try, Advent calendar.

You hid those **brown chocolate lumps** in your thin plastic bones and camouflaged it all in Christmas colors. Your perforated doors were locked shut and you teased us with larger and larger squares leading up to the big day.

But it got complicated.

We missed a couple days and then got two the next. Then we decided eating two was what we liked best. And that big door on Christmas Eve was too much to handle. So we ate all your chocolate in a big chocolate-eating scandal.

AWESOME!

The smell of a fresh Christmas tree

....

I grew up on artificial.

Whenever it was time to put up the tree, we'd clomp down to the basement and pull out the giant dented-and-torn cardboard box that looked like it'd been through a war and a washing machine. Inside was **a rat's nest** of jabby branches with faded spray-paint tags on the metal spokes. There were red for long ones, orange for medium, and yellow for the short bushy ones on top.

My sister and I would begin sorting branches before stabbing and twisting them into the stem. The end result was a **sparse Sears special** that looked like a cross between Charlie Brown's tree and one dying after a forest fire. It wasn't pretty, but by the time we drenched it in tinsel waterfalls, **construction paper loops**, and popcorn strings, it sure looked pretty to us.

Yes, fake was easier, **fake was free**, fake was the only way our tree could be.

But there was always something sweet about going to the neighbor's place and smelling the fresh pine from the freshly sawed tree in their living room. And I know those trees cost more, leave needles everywhere, and are chopping down nature.

But they sure smell a lot like Christmas.

And that smells a lot like

AWESOME!

Pulling out that old box of Christmas ornaments from when you were a kid

L et's go back.

Crack open that musty cardboard box from the basement storage space and get ready to brainwarp back to the **big eyes and bright lights** of your youth. Yes, yank out that twisted clump of yarn, ceramics, and construction paper and get ready for a sweet stroll down memory lane.

Hopefully your old box features some of these classics:

1. **A chipped ceramic you painted in elementary school.** Maybe it's the shiny Santa Claus that you doused in too much lacquer back in third grade. The brush-strokes make his beard look gray, and one of his eyeballs has a blue smear that makes him cross-

eyed. But his smile still holds and that little ribbon you knotted through his hat is perfect for hanging him back up on the tree.

2. **Homemade ornaments featuring some combination of construction paper, popcorn, and glitter.** When you were young you cleared off the kitchen table and set up a home workshop where you stitched popcorn, glued sparkles, and taped up little rolls of construction paper. And even though the reds have faded to orange and the glitter has cracked away, there's something beautiful about pulling out those squashed rings, baby handprints, or crayon drawings and letting your brain slip back to simpler days.

3. **The hundred-year-old hand-me-down.** You're lucky if you have one of these wood-carved gems bouncing around the bottom of the box. Someone's great-grandpa whittled a toy train engine or rosy-cheeked soldier from some softwood and delicately painted it to perfection. Maybe the tree it's carved from is two or three hundred years old and fell from the woods of a distant forest. High fives if you agree this beats the neon plastic from the dollar store any day.

Yes, when you pull out that box of Christmas ornaments from when you were a kid, it's like taking a magical mystery tour back to your childhood. It's a brief headtrip out of your serious grown-up body into the *Freaky Friday* **fun times** of yesterday.

AWESOME!

When construction cranes get Christmas lights on them

They're not selling anything.

Nope, Christmas lights on construction cranes just smile down on the city and cover us all in a warm and festive light. Flickering in the sky, **flashing way up high**, they hug us all together in a friendly yellow glow.

On top of that, it's sort of fun thinking about how they got there too. **Doesn't it seem kind of dangerous?** It's like someone risked their life just putting up lights for the people.

Thanks, Spider-Man!

AWESOME!

Finally finding the start of this stupid roll of tape

....

Y ou think it's gonna be easy.

But finally finding and finger-peeling the start of this stupid roll of tape takes two focused **hawk eyes**, a sharp set of witch's nails, and a soft and delicate touch.

If you're missing these you're outta luck.

But if you've got all three you're

AWESOME!

Looking through the little window in the oven

....

Where were you thirty-one thousand years ago? Immortal wizards aside, I'm guessing you were the same place I was: **nowhere**. Nope, you were just a twinkle in your cave-grandpa's eye back then. Seriously, you weren't around, but your ancestors were scraping across soggy jungles, wet cliffs, and dirty deserts trying to patch together an existence on hunted animals and handfuls of trees.

And then they discovered ovens.

People, it's true—according to our egghead pals over at Wikipedia, the **first ovens on earth** are from back around 29,000 BCE, when our cave families cooked mammoths outside their homemade huts.

So I say let's all stop for a second today and let our minds slip back to those cold desert plains.

Sharp winds whip dust across your **dirty face** on dark and dreary nights. Clouds crack and **cold drops fall** while you hear bushes scratching and footsteps stomping around you. Babies cry against sweaty chests, bleary eyes fade to rest, and everyone hunkers around one another for comfort and caring and touch . . .

Can you imagine how good it must have felt to cook up **some goooooooood eatin'** back in those prehistoric days? Yes, I'm guessing your entire pack salivated while crouching around the smoky fire.

Next time you look through that little window in the oven to scope your rising cupcakes, **bubbling lasagna**, or crisping cookies, don't forget to pay silent tribute to our past, when staring into the oven meant staring into energy . . . and life . . . and

AWESOME!

Flipping channels and stumbling on that one Christmas special you loved as a kid

....

It's a wonderful life.

When you're bunkering in the basement to get away from the holiday madness upstairs, it's always nice when the channel flipping pops you onto your favorite old flashback.

Which classic gem burrows into your heart?

* **That Rudolph stop-motion special.** Sam the Snowman (no relation to Frosty) narrates this epic tale of outcasts Rudolph and Hermey the Elf as they stumble through the North Pole meeting Yukon Cornelius and the Abominable Snowman before taking refuge on the Island of Misfit Toys. Never forget the moral of the story: Follow your heart and become a dentist.

* *A Charlie Brown Christmas.* Like most Charlie Brown cartoons, this one features monotone voices, confusing plots, and dry humor. Thank-

fully, jazzy piano music and dancing kids make it all come together.

* **Any non-Christmas movie that takes place during Christmas.** Sure, Bruce Willis crawling around office ducts in *Die Hard* might not *seem* festive, but listen closely to the background music and you'll see it deserves its place up here. We'll throw in *Lethal Weapon*, *Gremlins*, and *Batman Returns* too.

* *How the Grinch Stole Christmas.* All the Whos living in Whoville have a serious problem in that there's a freakish monster living in the cliffs above their romantic mountain town. He is dramatically reducing property values by the day. If you don't love the big rhyming sing-a-long finish to this one, then your heart is officially three sizes too small.

* *Frosty the Snowman.* Poor Frosty just doesn't have the personality of Sam the Snowman from the Rudolph special. And since they always air this one with Rudolph, the inferiority of Frosty jumps out even more. Honestly, if Frosty is your favorite old Christmas special, then I feel sorry for you. You had a rough childhood.

* **Whatever special is on the same time as *Frosty* on the other channel.** *A Garfield Christmas, John Denver*

and the Muppets, or *Will Vinton's Claymation Christmas* automatically win.

* ***It's a Wonderful Life*** when you stumble on this old faithful classic.

Finding your favorite holiday special from when you were a kid on TV is like uncovering a hidden stash of buried treasure at the bottom of the sea. It doesn't matter if you've seen it a hundred times, have it on your computer, or own the DVD either. There's just something sweet about feeling like it was waiting there at this very moment and the stars just aligned to make it happen.

AWESOME!

Eating the first freshly baked cookie from the oven even though it's way too hot

It burns.

Chocolate chips drip down your fingertips as that **softly crumbling cookie** melts into a hot puddle of steamy goodness in the middle of your mouth. Gasp for air, **pop your eyes**, and suck in some cool breaths as you try to chew without touching that red-hot cookie lava.

Part of what makes these cookies delicious is that you can't buy them at the store. Nope, cellophane stacks of **paper-wrapped packs** got nothing on the hot crumbly oozing across the burning pan. Remember, you sweated up a storm in the kitchen for these, cracking eggs, **melting butter**, and beating the wet floury mixture into a sticky brown pulp. You slaved away for the Christmas cookie trade and piled 'em high before the in-laws came over.

Now is not the time to wait.

Now is the time to enjoy it.

AWESOME!

When the wrapping paper lines up perfectly when you go to tape it

....

Wrapping is serious.

Yes, somewhere between peeling tape, snipping corners, and curling ribbons, you start obsessing over all the little details. And sure, if you're like me your present just ends up a **corner-dented patchwork** of twisted tape and shoddy edges. But for the pros there's something sweet about getting the whole thing looking *jusssssssssst* right.

UNAWESOME!

AWESOME!

Forgetting you ordered a gift online and then having it randomly show up

··

G oodbye, perfume.

When I was a little kid I dreaded walking through **Perfume Alley** at the front of the department store. Holding my mom's or dad's hand, I'd squeeze my face real tight while walking past lipstick-smeared smilies standing in front of shiny glass-n-brass countertops holding tiny square Weapons of Mass Irritation.

Yes, I dreaded those long walks through **Stink Jungle**, but they seemed necessary at the time. After all, sheets and toys and clothes for boys were all stationed behind those invisible clouds of strong smells and toddler migraines.

In those days there wasn't an option.

But in these days it's different.

Click, click, you're done. *Click, click*, that was fun. *Click, click*, back to reruns.

And when you turn off the computer, when you shut off that screen, when you put away your wallet, when you leave the machine—well, if you're like me one thing happens immediately.

You completely forget about it.

So whether it's new books or concert tickets or video games or cricket wickets, the point is that you forget it's coming and you forget you bought it. This is the beauty of shopping in **Your Own Smell**, folks. Soon a day passes, then another, then another one passes, and then a package arrives . . .

And what a surprise!

In a cardboard disguise!

It's a feast for the eyes!

That makes you scream to the skies!

AWESOME!

The Holiday Party Save

Do we need all those parties?

Sure, we all love catching up with close friends in **Christmas sweaters**, but sometimes the office party feels like a meeting with veggie trays, and clinking drinks with second cousins gets old. Face it—there are times when you need to be saved, my friends. Yes, the **Holiday Party Save** happens anytime a friend yanks you from a bad holiday party conversation by pulling off a thrilling and daring rescue mission.

Here's how it all goes down:

Step 1: **The Plan.** Say tonight you're heading to your uncle's annual Christmas party with your new boyfriend. As you both walk into Stranger Conversation Territory, it's important to make that deal up front: You save them, they save you. Don't forget to shake.

Step 2: **The Signal.** You're trapped! When you find yourself listening to never-ending vacation stories, getting detailed stock-picking advice, or hearing about someone's thesis, it's time to get out. Signal your friend with an eager Smile 'n' Raised Eyebrows glance, casual Nodding Head-Tilt beckon, or if absolutely necessary, a booming bloodcurdling "Get over here!" scream, like Scorpion in *Mortal Kombat*.

Step 3: The Save. Here's the tricky part. Your friend comes over and has two options. First, they can play **False Emergency** and drag you away while apologizing to the chatty strangers. This is risky because it could look forced and you'll need to disappear rather than just talk to someone else. Instead, they can try **The Natural**, which is where they drop a nice, normal transition into the conversation. "Should we go grab some food?" "Linda just got here, let's say hi," or "Where's the bathroom?" usually work well.

Remember: When you're stuck, **when you're stranded**, when all you see is gloom, just yell for your brothers and sisters and let them pull you across the room.

AWESOME!

Driving around town to see all the Christmas lights

E very city has a street.

It's the quiet cul-de-sac where all the neighbors play it big for Christmas and decorate their homes with the greatest light show the world has ever seen. Word gets out through the local paper or radio station and soon everyone knows it's just the place to go for a late night cruise down **Neon Light Lane.**

It's the one place everyone enjoys traffic jams.

Sitting bumper to bumper around the quiet crescent, you push your hat above your forehead, **press your mittens to the window**, and stare out at the twinkling scene. Reds and greens flicker and flash on your darkened face as snow reflects classy floodlights, roofs beam with strings of white, and inflatable Santas bob and wave from the middle of lawns.

And there's always one house that is just a bit better than the rest. It's probably the family that got the parade route started with the big splash every year. I like thinking the neighbors leaned on their shovels with furrowed brows when they first saw lights spelling *Merry Christmas* being draped across the roof, but over time their Grinch-like hearts melted and they felt the Christmas spirit themselves.

Somehow over time the street grew and grew and grew until it became the sparkly beauty we see today. There's something fun and something sweet about bundling up and just driving down the street. Hear the carols softly on the radio, **feel the smiles in the car**, and take a moment to relax and remember how lucky we are.

AWESOME!

Wrapping a gift to make it look like something else

··

I was a mystery gifter.

Yes, when I was little I would throw a **handful of rocks** in a cardboard box from Sears together with a handwritten note saying "Free backrub!" or "This piece of paper entitles the bearer to me cleaning their room." My sister, Nina, would shake my **mystery box** under the tree before she excitedly opened it on Christmas morning.

Of course, most of the time she was disappointed to find she was ruthlessly deceived, but my homemade gift certificates generally made up for it. "You know, that wasn't very nice of you," she'd say as I **karate-chopped** her shoulder blades. "Ooohhh, right there, right there. Bit lower. Mmmm."

Nina and my parents got into the game over time and I began receiving gift cards wrapped in jewel cases and Sega Game Gear games wrapped to look like a tie.

Wrapping a gift to make it look like something else helps keep the surprise a surprise. It's a fun way to save some excitement for the day and sprinkles Christmas morning with a surprising little dose of

AWESOME!

The Super Present Power Shop

Y ou're running late.

When it's almost Christmas and there's nothing under the tree, it's time to furrow your brows, steady your glare, and clench those fists for a big Super Present Power Shop.

Yes, this is where you burst into the mall in a **sweatshirt-and-running-shoes tornado** and spin around at high speeds until successfully finding something for everyone on your list.

Black Friday's long gone, online delivery windows are closed, and now it's crunch time. Here are some tips to pulling it off:

- **Good parkin' is good startin'.** Circling the frozen tundra in lot WW is a fool's game. No, you need to find the secret YMCA entrance, get a drop-off and pickup, or arrive ten minutes before doors open to score a front spot. Don't forget the Parking Lot Pull Through.
- **Skip the coat, grab the kicks.** Leave your winter jacket in the trunk and sprint across the icy lot to the front

door, because thirty seconds of frozen lungs is worth avoiding three hours of overheating. Plus, those running shoes will help you run and dive for the last Baby Farts-A-Lot in the toy store.

- **Plug in.** Stuff some headphones in your ears and rock out to 2 Unlimited or Technotronic to stay motivated. Remember: Nothing slows you down more than hearing "Santa Baby" for the third time in an hour, so pump up the jam and let's move this.

- **Couples for couples.** If you have couples on your list, just divide the number of gifts by two. Beer mug for him, wineglasses for her? No, martini shaker for both. You get the idea.

- **Close your list, open your mind.** Focus is important, so jot down your names and ideas before hitting the stores. Just make sure to leave your mind open for things to jump off the shelves. Breath mints, *People* magazines, and IKEA golf pencils all make lovely stocking stuffers.

- **Bag a monster.** It's important to ask the first store you visit for the largest bags they have. They should go fishing for a couple minutes and pull out the king-sized ones normally reserved for toaster ovens and dehumidifiers. Use that monster to eat everything else you buy all day.

Okay, listen, listen—these are just a few tips to get you going. As you start perfecting your Power Shop you'll grow more advanced techniques, like stuffing your pockets with peanut butter sandwiches, phoning for inventory checks while waiting in lines, and **buying someone a sled** so you can drag all your presents from shop to shop.

But no matter what kind of Power Shop you pull off, one thing's for sure: When you crash back into your couch surrounded by full bags and a crossed-off list, well . . . it's time to unclench your muscles, **droop your eyes**, and smile slowly at your mall-conquering moment of

AWESOME!

When there's no line at the mall to meet Santa Claus

....

D id you sit on Santa when you were a kid?

If so, I'm guessing your festive picture doesn't show the two hours your parents waited in **Cardboard Candyland** lineups for you to jump on his lap. Crying babies by the food court and toddler pee on the carpeted floor are cropped out of your magical memory.

But they were there!

When there's no line to meet Santa, it means your Saturday can keep chugging without a blistering headache in the middle of the mall. So get your kid on that knee and photoflash that big smile, because the holidays are busy and it's time to keep moving and keep grooving, baby.

AWESOME!

Just barely wrapping a gift with that tiny scrap of leftover paper

....

Thanks, jewelry box, **random bar of soap**, and chocolate orange.

You came through in the clutch to help use the final shredded scrap of wrap.

AWESOME!

Real bearded Santas

Rare is the Santa Claus who can earnestly grow that full lion's mane of bright white hair. But I'm sorry, it's what **We The People** demand. Fake beards on Santa Claus are an insult. They mock the jolly Christmas cheer, like a wreath made out of lettuce, a gingerbread house made of saltines, or a turkey made out of Tofurky.

So let's get one thing straight, Kringle: Grow the real beard or don't apply at the mall.

It's that simple.

AWESOME!

Nailing the perfect move in a board game on Christmas Eve

....

Holiday time is board game time.

I think it's because there's just something quiet and old-fashioned about opening the dusty closet and pulling out the old family favorites from yesteryear. With ages spread across the spectrum, board games are a great equalizer. Plus, buzzing ringtones and email beeps fade to silence as families across the country cuddle up to open those old boxes. **Pencils with broken leads**, yellowed instructions, and faded homemade scorecards litter the box and make it look like that clattery **kitchen drawer** of assorted knickknacks. Take a deep breath and sniff up a familiar musty scent that takes you way, way back.

Now personally, I'm terrible at board games.

Look at me: trying to roll doubles to bust outta jail, putting down *bill* or *door* on a no-word score, and frantically stabbing my pencil at my scribbly drawing over and over while the hourglass sand drips down. You see, this is why I love those rare moments when even I manage to nail a perfect board game move during Family Night. Settle down beside the

Christmas tree, pour a glass of eggnog, and grab a plate of homemade cookies before going back with some of these classic moves:

10. **When your brother challenges a word you made up in Scrabble and it ends up being a real word.** Thanks for your giant, nonsensical vocabulary, *Scrabble Dictionary*. We'll take *op*, *pe*, or *xi* to the bank any day.

9. **Eating the last marble in Hungry Hungry Hippos.** When the game begins it's a gobble, gobble, give Mom a headache feeding frenzy. But when there's only one white marble spinning around, everything turns into goosebump-popping, eyebrow-furrowing strategy and wit. Make your move and calmly splash back into the river.

8. **Suddenly noticing you got a surprise diagonal in Connect Four.** When you realize you won the game, make sure you throw your nose in the air, give a slow and evil smile, and calmly pet your cat. This was your plan all along.

7. **Becoming a doctor in The Game of LIFE.** When you land on the top salary spot, you're laughing for the rest of the game. Just make sure your station wagon doesn't topple off the side of the mountain, spilling your pink and blue kids everywhere.

6. **When your mom figures out that bumpy lump of purple clay you're molding in Cranium is actually a cheeseburger.** Good work, Michelangelo.

5. **Guessing your Grandma's Mastermind combination in three tries.** Even though it's usually a fluke, make sure you take a minute to stare absently at the Ping-Pong table and daydream about life as a professional code breaker.

4. **Actually using the horse to kill off a major player in chess.** That legless knight never seems very powerful until the moment you realize he's in trampling distance of a big kill. Make sure you use the piece to purposefully whack your opponent across the room and, for extra fun, let out an obnoxious whinny.

3. **Using the stock answer for a Trivial Pursuit category and getting the pie piece.** Thanks for saving the day, Michael Jordan, Marlon Brando, or nitrogen.

2. **Coming up with a lie so good in Balderdash that when they're all read out you almost believe your own definition is the real one.** You're at the top of your game, so enjoy the moment and get ready to reel in some suckers.

1. **Rolling double sixes in Monopoly and landing after the other guy's Park Place and Boardwalk hotels.** Good move skipping the five-star joints in favor of crash-

ing on Baltic Avenue. The kids didn't need a swimming pool or HBO anyway.

People, you know it and I know it: These Perfect Board
Game Moments can change the game and knock your sister
straight outta the living room. They're beautiful little breaks
in the middle of tense moments that fill holiday Family
Night with a great big shot of

AWESOME!

Staring into a fire

· ·

Check out the sun.

It's just a big ball of fire swirling high in the sky.

Plants, heat, life, pretty sunsets—damn girl, that's some good deals for free.

Yes, we owe a lot to that friendly fireball, so it's no wonder one of the **Greatest Things We Ever Did** was make fire in its likeness here on Earth. So first up, let's just stop for a moment today and close our eyes to say, "Good job, cavemen."

Now these days whether you're sitting on a wet log around a smoky campfire, cuddling on the couch on Christmas Eve, or cooking up dinner on the grill, it sure is easy to get mesmerized by the flames.

Stare into the red-hot heat as it crackles and pops before your eyes. Watch as licks and curls **unfurl and swirl** in a twisted dance of fiery flames. Let the heat wash over you as those beautiful shapes flicker in a never-ending show of lights. There is a rhythm and beat to the movement, but at the same time it's just . . . natural and free.

Staring into a fire warms your eyes . . . and your heart. Sometimes it comes with tea and hot chocolate, **squished slippers**, and good conversation. Sometimes it comes with ocean waves and wind whispering through trees under a dimming pink sky. Sometimes it comes at the cottage, sometimes it comes at the park, sometimes it comes in the morning, sometimes it comes when it's dark . . .

But whenever you're lucky enough to **transplant your brain** to the center of the flames, it's always an escape from the world . . . and always an escape into

AWESOME!

When the Christmas tree gives the only light in the room

··

Turn out the lights.

Pull the curtains open and watch as **jumbo snowflakes** drift past the window, snow-covered kids walk by dragging sleds, and winter winds whisper through the evergreens.

Smell the turkey crisping in the oven, listen to scratchy carols spinning in your head, and hear footsteps from the family slowly come together in front of the sparkling tree . . .

Swipe your daughter's bangs as she lies in your lap, smile at Grandpa sipping eggnog on the ottoman, or cuddle up with your cousins in a pile of cozy blankets and comfy sweats on the couch.

Sip that crystal glass of eggnog, **sniff the pine of the tree**, and relax and share a quiet moment of bliss with someone touching your hands . . . or your heart.

AWESOME!

When you can actually
hear it snowing

....

Just listen.

When the white sky splits and the **big flakes fall**, there's a certain peaceful calm that covers everything like a blanket. Floating flurries flutter and fly past **dull yellow streetlamps** before covering coats and cars in a thin layer of icing. Whistling winds fade to whispers and street beeps get muffled into the slowed-down scene in front of you.

Yes, when snowflakes blow **those brake lights glow** and everything slows into

AWESOME!

Waking up and realizing it's Christmas

....

After waiting and wait-

ing and waiting and waiting and waiting and waiting and
waiting and waiting and waiting and waiting and waiting
and waiting and waiting and waiting and waiting and wait-
ing and waiting and waiting and waiting and waiting and
waiting and waiting and waiting and waiting and waiting
and waiting and waiting and waiting and waiting and wait-
ing and waiting and waiting and waiting and waiting and
waiting and waiting and waiting and waiting and waiting
and waiting and waiting and waiting and waiting and wait-
ing and waiting and waiting and waiting and waiting and
waiting and waiting and waiting and waiting and waiting
and waiting and waiting and waiting and waiting and wait-
ing and waiting and waiting and waiting and waiting and
waiting and waiting and waiting and waiting and waiting
and waiting and waiting and waiting and waiting and wait-
ing and waiting and waiting and waiting and waiting and
waiting and waiting and waiting and waiting and waiting
and waiting and waiting and waiting and waiting and wait-
ing and waiting and waiting and waiting and waiting and
waiting and waiting and waiting and waiting and waiting
and waiting and waiting and waiting and waiting and wait-
ing and waiting and waiting and waiting and waiting and
waiting and waiting and waiting and waiting and waiting
and waiting and waiting and waiting and waiting and wait-
ing and waiting and waiting and waiting and waiting and

waiting and waiting and waiting and waiting and waiting . . .
It's finally here.

AWESOME!

Ripping your present open like a wild animal

....

First, some apologies.

We're sorry, **Endurance Wrapper**. You spent thirty minutes getting the present just right with your scissor-frilled ribbons, crisply folded corners, and those adorable little bows. You put time in and we didn't respect that with our raccoon-with-rabies slaughtering of your gift.

We're sorry, **Auntie Paper Collector**. We know you quietly collect all the discarded bows and paper and fold it into little piles to use for next year. Nobody minds the creased 1990s sun-faded reindeer wrapping paper because we know you're saving money and the planet. But this time we didn't leave you with much. Unless you're collecting saliva-smeared scraps, squashed boxes, and torn bows.

We're sorry, **Garbage Collecting Dad**. We see you trudging around the family room with the World's Lightest Garbage Bag, scooping up all the tiny bits of tissue paper and sticky ripped price tags. We know your job would be a lot easier if all presents moved to a Gift Bag Only Policy.

We are very, very sorry to you all.

And now that we've apologized our conscience is clear.

Because the truth is we love ripping open presents like a drugged-up reindeer.

AWESOME!

When the gift receipt is already in the box

··

A *LF* was a great TV show.

But let's be honest—you may not want to own the wisecracking, **cat-eating alien's** first three seasons on DVD.

So if you land *ALF*, or a shot glass chess set, or a gelato maker, or a sweater that doesn't fit you, or the **Classic Concentration board game**, then you may find yourself saying, "Oh thank you, it's just what I always wanted," when you're actually thinking, *Oh thank you, it's just what I never wanted.*

That's why it's great when you see the gift receipt just lying in the box after you pull out the gift. You avoid the awkward "It's okay if you don't like it" (**No, no, I do**), "I wasn't sure if it was something you wanted" (**No, no, it is**), "They have it in black too if you don't like green" (**No, no, I like green**), or "I can give you the receipt if you don't like it" (**No, no, I like it**) conversations.

Yes, when the gift receipt is already in the box, there are

no questions asked, no questions answered. It's just sitting there, **a secret wink**, a private head nod, a quiet understanding between you and the very kind, very generous, very thought-ful person who gave you the present.

AWESOME!

Trying on your new clothes as soon as you unwrap them

....

S tiff creases, **unhemmed pants**, and itchy tags can't dent your mood.

Now it's time to change real fast, **clear the kitchen runway**, and strut your stuff in a private fashion show for your friends and family.

And dog.

AWESOME!

Staying in your pajamas all day

··

It's a rare treat.

Maybe it's that lazy Sunday after Christmas with a hot coffee, fat paper, and **dusty sunlight** beaming through the windows. Or maybe it's the Friday sick day where you leave the glasses on, tie the ponytail up, and lounge around in a robe watching soaps with the cat. Or maybe it's Christmas Day after presents, cuddling up with the kids and watching movies before turkey dinner.

Sure, sometimes you wake up without firm plans to stay in your pajamas all day. Maybe you have some errands, a lunch date, or a grocery list. But sometimes those plans hit the ground and you pass **The Pajama Point of No Return**—that moment where you suddenly realize you're too close to bedtime to worry about getting ready for the day.

Yes, once in a while, **once in a moment**, maybe just once a year, it's fun to have a super chilled-out lazy **You Day** full of peaceful relaxing in some warm and comfy clothes.

AWESOME!

The In-law Nap

··

The In-law Nap is any nap you manage to pull off at the in-law's house. As long as it's not during Thanksgiving dinner, **Christmas present unwrapping**, or while the birthday cake is served, it is a completely legal nap and fully counts as spending quality time visiting the in-laws.

Whether you skip out on setting the table, **ditch helping with the dishes**, or just miss a couple hours playing cards with Grandma . . . it doesn't matter.

All that matters is you pulled it off.

Yes, you answered a **phony cell phone call** in the other room for twenty minutes, you snuck into the kids' fort and fell asleep in the cushion barracks, or you hid on a pile of jackets and **scraggly blankets** in the spare bedroom.

All that matters is you pulled it off.

All that matters is that you're

AWESOME!

Drinking with Grandma

It's time for some intergenerational egg nogging.

Get ready to light the Yule log, **sail the gravy boat**, and get your eighty-five-pound grandmother a sloshy glass of rummy nog.

Now, whatever your age, whatever your tastes, whatever your pleasures, whatever your fates, let's all agree on one thing today: Grabbing an occasional festive drink with **your mom's mom** or your son's son bridges boundaries and crosses divides.

Once upon a time, your grandma used to boogie. Once upon a time, your grandma threw it down. Yes, I'm saying before you danced on tables, she danced on them too. And before you learned to twist off, she was guzzling brews.

So when the holidays hit and the families combine, it's time to **bring out the punch bowl** and time to have a good time. Because we're not here forever and we're not here very long.

We don't get many chances, so toss one back before Granny's gone.

I never knew my grandparents, but I heard stories they were great . . . so I know if they were here we'd party hard before it got too late.

AWESOME!

Putting a Santa hat on your pet or grandparent

It's party time.

And those Christmas sweaters are just the beginning.

I mean sure, tossing on a **thick woolly** for the holiday party is a sure way to spread the cheer—especially if your sweater features hypnotic swirls of red and green, **a giant floating snowman head**, or an intense action sequence of Santa flying his reindeer through a blizzard.

But to really get that party going and that **eggnog flowing**, you've got to crank it up a notch. Yes, we're talking about tossing a Santa cap on your golden retriever or Grandpa, we're talking about tossing one on your Labradoodle or Grandma, and we're talking about everyone donning their **gay apparel** to whip this holiday bash into a whole new level of

AWESOME!

Sucking in your stomach just before the family photo is taken

....

When someone whips out a camera, it's time to suck it in, baby. Eye the trigger finger and pull in when they push down. After all, maybe there's a six-pack under that stained and baggy T-shirt. I mean, we have no reason to suspect a jiggly bowl of **jelly belly** or anything.

There's just no proof.

AWESOME!

Drinking anything besides wine out of a wineglass

··

Suddenly your milk gets classy, your orange juice gets refined, and your **chocolate milk** feels more sophisticated. When you're a kid you suddenly go from ten years old to thirty and can legally show up at **The Kids Table** with heavily slicked and parted hair, a handkerchief puffing out of your pocket, and cuff links.

AWESOME!

Taking off your pants after the fourth helping

· ·

Cavemen didn't wear jeans.

Nope, hiding from mammoths, **bashing saber-toothed skulls**, and setting up the cave was tough enough without furry leg warmers chafing their hairy thighs.

And it wasn't just them either: Free-legs living was **The Thing To Do** for the past hundred thousand years, until a bunch of horse-riding Persians invented pants back in the sixth century BCE. Presumably, they were sick of getting **back-of-the-horse burn** from bumpy rides and frustrated with the poor selection of creams and lotions at their local Megamart. But hey, if you were riding horses in the nude, I'm sure you'd agree with wearing all pants all the time too.

Flash forward to today and pants are a massive worldwide hit. Everywhere you go, everywhere you look, it's pants, pants, pants. Togas, kilts, skirts—they tried, they tried, but they just couldn't find the secret key to international popularity.

Nowadays we wear pants for warmth at the ice rink, **hygiene on the subway car**, or denim paper towels in the basement bathroom bar.

But even though they're handy and helpful, pants have a

downside too: Yes, I'm talking about crotch creases, tight belts, and ass-jammy wallets all day. Sure, maybe you're used to them, maybe you've accepted pants-wearing, but maybe sometimes . . . sometimes . . . sometimes . . . they just get in the way.

If you're with me, say hey.

If you're with me, stop today.

If you're with me . . . it's okay.

Because you know how great it feels enjoying that moment of sweet release when your legs finally bust free of the shackles of everyday living. When you finish that fourth helping of Christmas dinner, it's time to slap open the heavy buckle, **unzip that tight fly**, and collapse backward onto your couch as you sloppily kick-peel that pair of tight jeans down and off your fabulous legs.

Just maybe wait for Grandma to go home first.

Next time you take your pants off, make sure to stop for a moment and let your legs see the light . . . **let them feel the air** . . . and let them enjoy being beautifully free and naked and

AWESOME!

When your guests do the dishes even after you told them not to

It's time for Christmas dinner.

Yes, sweaty and flushed, you run around **baking bread** and breaking eggs before that doorbell *bing-bong*s, the guests ping-pong, and everyone sits down to eat up your delicious holiday meal.

Of course, you enjoy the dinner—you love it, it's great— but you don't **really** enjoy it. No, you're running around refilling glasses, folding napkins, scooping seconds, warming pies. You're cleaning crumbs, wiping babies, and keeping an eye on The Kids Table. While everyone sits and chats, you're a **Tasmanian devil** of dining room insanity, whipping into a whirlwind and making sure everyone enjoys their meal.

By the end, you're completely and utterly exhausted. Your bones are bleeding, your skin is stinging, and your body is aching for a tender hug from a cushy couch.

That's why it's great when your guests offer to do the dishes after the meal.

"No, no, no," you say. "Sit down, sit down, sit down."

But they insist, but you insist, **but they insist**, but you insist,

but they insist . . . and then finally you just stare back at them with hollow, broken eyes and give up.

Now you crash-land on the couch, listening to carols as your guests fill the sink and bubble up the suds. And what a beautiful moment of sweet relief it is when you walk back in there and see everything sparklingly clean.

Plus, for the rest of the week you get to enjoy the Treasure Hunt that comes with finding your own dishes in all the wrong cupboards. But it's no big deal, so just smile and enjoy those Gravy Boat Rescue Missions and Wooden Spoon Search Parties with a smile.

Yes, this one goes out to guests who wash the dishes even after we told them not to. Today we say thanks for the love, **thanks for the memories**, and thanks for scrubbing the crusty stuffing dish.

AWESOME!

Successfully regifting a present to someone who wants it

....

W hat do cellophane-wrapped mugs of mini candy canes, **Season 3 of *Mr. Belvedere* on VHS**, and framed photos of someone else's dog have in common?

They're just what we never wanted.

But that's okay, that's okay—because someone else might! Yes, now it's time for some **Regifting Magic**, people. It's time to regift like you've never regifted before. You're a regifting machine if you follow these three steps to freedom:

1. **Smile sweetly.** Never look a gift horse in the mouth. Instead, look them in the eyes while saying thank you over and over. You may also find it helpful to practice these lines (for these items): "I've been meaning to try that place!" (gift card to Taco Bell), "How did you know I liked this shade of green?!" (puke green sweater), and "It's perfect, it's perfect— honestly, how have I even been wearing shoes all these years?!" (shoehorn).

2. **Add it to your gifts-to-give pile.** When you get home, make sure to write a thank-you card promptly and then toss the gift in the closet with your motorized self-twirling spaghetti fork, Streetlamps of the World page-a-day calendar, and novelty light-up ceramic angel. Let your inventory bulk up a bit so you've got good regift variety, and be sure to hide the stash from future regiftees. Post-it Notes with the name of the person who gave it to you can also help prevent the dreaded Boomerang Gift. Don't let it happen to you.

3. **Annnnnnd . . . regift!** Remember that one man's trash is another man's treasure. When you look at it this way, it feels like you're doing very important gift-giving charity work. You're a misfit present coordinator! Now, you need to be about 90 percent sure the regiftee will love the present. After all, there's nothing wrong with gift cards to Taco Bell and light-up ceramic angels. It's just that one goes to your backward-cap skateboarding rascal of a little cousin and the other goes to your grandma who loves tacos.

AWESOME!

When they finally stop playing Christmas songs on the radio

....

B ecause at some point we all stop caring what Bing Crosby is dreaming about.

AWESOME!

When the in-laws leave

Now, now.

Don't get us wrong.

It's great filling the home with hugs and love and holiday joy. Everyone loves grandpas and grandmas and brand-new toys. Yes, family fills living rooms with laughter, basements with board games, and kitchens with kisses.

But let's be honest—holiday guests come with a bit of holiday stress too.

Mall hopping and last-minute shopping, **wrapping boxes of fancy chocolates**, cooking suppers without taking uppers—yes, it adds up to memories and it adds up to fun, but we're saying it's also okay when the visit is done.

It's beautiful opening your hearts and your home to the people you love.

But it's beautiful kissing goodbye and getting your place back too.

AWESOME!

Getting seven more days of presents than your friends who celebrate Christmas

How's your Hanukkah education?

Forgive me, but mine needs brushing up, so here goes.

Hanukkah is an eight-night celebration that includes lighting the candles of the menorah (candleholder), **playing with the dreidel** (four-sided spinning die), eating latkes (home-made McDonald's hash browns), receiving Hanukkah gelt (cash or chocolate coins), and scoring presents.

See, about two thousand years ago a Syrian king named Antiochus IV began to outlaw Jewish religious practices. As if having a Roman numeral in his name weren't badass enough, this guy had his henchmen trash a **Jewish temple in Jerusalem** and erect an idol of a Greek god there. Look, I don't know where you stand on religion, but I think we can all agree that building your own church right on top of someone else's isn't very nice.

Some Jewish folks took exception and began a famous rebellion where they fought back and reclaimed the temple. They wanted to rededicate it, but couldn't find enough oil to light the menorah. They needed a few bottles of the good stuff but only found one, so they just said, "Oh well, whatever!" and used it up.

Miracle of miracles, the one bottle of oil **lasted eight nights**, which gave them time to produce more oil. This is why Hanukkah takes place over eight days and each night is commemorated by lighting the eight candles of the menorah one by one.

And just think about that for a second.

Eight nights!

These days, a lot of Jewish folks trade gifts every night of the holiday. And though it's clearly not just what the holiday is about, there's something sweet about giving presents, **trading love**, and showing your family how much they mean to you for eight days in a row.

So today we say thank you, oil miracle of thousands of years ago.

Thank you for giving us seven more days of gifts than our friends.

AWESOME!

Eating anything
with oil in it

I was chatting with my friend Jon the other day and he said his favorite part of Hanukkah is the fact that the holiday embraces eating anything with oil in it. "See, we're celebrating the oil lasting eight days," he said, smiling. "So we deep-fry the crap out of everything in the name of religious freedom."

Hey, that seems like a great way to justify a wobbly tower of **potato latkes** to me. I love those greasy little pancakes of grated potatoes, egg, and flour just as much as I love jelly-filled donuts, which are conveniently another Hanukkah treat.

But by Jon's count, if we're celebrating the grease there should be no stopping there. We started talking about funnel cakes, **french fries**, and those deep-fried Mars bars you find at the fair. We talked about extra-crispy chicken, **gooey**

mozzarella sticks, and those fish and chips that soak through the paper bag.

Eating anything with oil in it is a great way to enjoy Hanukkah.

So let's all tuck in a napkin and celebrate.

AWESOME!

When your gelt melts perfectly in your mouth instead of in the wrapper

Kids get gelt for Hanukkah. It comes in the form of presents, cash, or **gold foil-wrapped chocolate coins** that look like they came from a birthday loot bag. Nope, they can't fit into a slot machine or be traded for goods and services, but those little chocolate coins are great for gambling in dreidel games or just gobbling right up.

Unfortunately, the chocolate has a tendency to melt in warm hands, hot rooms, or sunny backyards. And nobody likes slow-peeling the **melty brown surprise** and licking the messy chocolate out of it. It's just too much work for some foil-tasting chocolate and tongue cuts.

But that's why it's a beautiful moment when your gelt melts perfectly in your mouth instead of in the wrapper.

Happy Hanukkah, tongue.

AWESOME!

Drinking from the same cup
as all your relatives

....

How's your Kwanzaa education?

Forgive me, but mine needs brushing up, so here goes.

Kwanzaa is a weeklong holiday, from December 26th to January 1st each year, honoring African-American heritage and culture. Like most other holidays, the theme once again is parties and plenty of them. Lighting candles, **swapping presents**, and feasting like mad are part of the fun.

Now, Kwanzaa isn't steeped in traditions from **thousands of years ago**. Nope, a guy named Ron Karenga just up and invented Kwanzaa in 1966! Poof, just like that—one year, no Kwanzaa, the next year, Kwanzaa. Let's let him inspire all future Holiday Inventors of the world! Ron said he just wanted to "give Blacks an opportunity to celebrate themselves and their history." So he wrote down a list of seven principles that each of the seven days are meant to honor:

unity, **self-determination**, collective work and responsibility, cooperative economics, purpose, creativity, and faith.

These days, Kwanzaa is a big party with ceremonies including decorating your house with colorful cloths and fresh fruit, wishing one another a "Joyous Kwanzaa!" and drinking from a big shared cup called a **Kikombe cha Umoja**. This is a nicely decorated cup filled with wine or **grape juice**, and it's passed from oldest to youngest at the dinner party, with each person saying a blessing to the person before them.

I say drinking from the same cup as all your relatives is a great idea for a few big reasons:

1. **Catch the cold.** Because when the six-year-old brings a runny nose and sneezes home from kindergarten, we're all getting it anyway. May as well get exposed to the bugs from the get-go instead of dragging out the pain.

2. **Muzzle crazy uncles.** Now instead of pouring their fifth glass of wine and getting into long-winded conspiracy theory rants, they'll be forced to share a cup of grape juice with the teens.

3. **Fewer dishes for Grandma.** Instead of slaving over a sink full of dirty cups and wineglasses, she'll just put her feet up and enjoy a Kwanzaa Coma as we

all spill into the basement for video games and Ping-Pong.

Drinking from the same cup as all your relatives on Kwanzaa is a beautiful moment.

So keep passing it around and sipping up the AWESOME!

Knowing that your holiday is worth more Scrabble points than any other holiday

....

Sorry, Christmas, Hanukkah, Diwali, Eid, and Easter. Kwanzaa's got you beat.

Triple word or bust.

AWESOME!

The sound of a cork popping

Here comes the party.

When you hear the champagne cork pop out and the **bubbly start fizzing**, it means it's time for some wet pours and lots of bubbles in the glass. We're not first class, just a rowdy gang of friends looking to bring in the new year with a great night.

Let's get started.

AWESOME!

Watching bartenders work really fast

....

It's more than a pour.

Watching a bartender work really fast is like staring through **the factory glass** and seeing all the whirring parts bump and grind before your beautiful finished drink pops out. Yes, you're the foreman in a hard hat standing with **a clipboard and a smile** watching all the bells ring, **springs spring**, and assembly lines ding before a glass full of ice, cherries, and umbrellas appears before your eyes.

Now, there are some key moves mastered by most really, really fast bartenders:

1. **Throwing things.** There's no time to place the bottle cap in the trash can, so it's important to fling it off the mirror and let it Plinko down between all the vodka and peach schnapps bottles on the bar.

2. **Absolutely no talking.** In a way really, really fast bartenders are like really, really fast mimes. Usually they'll raise their eyebrows or put their ear in for the order and then immediately start slicing lemons, stirring glasses, and squeezing taps without

speaking. Black clothes and painted teardrops are optional, unless you're in a goth bar.

3. **No official measurements.** Forget the rules, because really, really fast bartenders trust their eyeballs and know their mix ratios cold.

4. **The Lineup Pour.** When you order three of the same drink, it's a classic move to squeeze the glasses together and just fill them up in one slowly moving pour. This move goes up a notch when their free hand is popping lemon wedges on the rim too. Watch out for sloppy bar puddles.

Yes, when you watch a bartender work really fast, you're seeing an expert in action. Bands play and people scream while they move in almost silent worlds in the middle of loud crowds. Eyes are focused, **feet are fleet**, and hands are steady in these beautifully intense scenes of quick pours, **expert fills**, and fast and furious moments of

AWESOME!

Saying "See you next year!" to everyone on New Year's Eve and then laughing hysterically

. . . .

You crack us up.
     Never stop being you.
AWESOME!

Actually knowing more than three words of that New Year's song

··

L isten up, songwriters.

It's high time one of you grabbed a pen and paper and scribbled out a new song for New Year's. Because when the ball drops and the **glasses clink**, we're all standing between streamers stumbling through a few words from "Auld Lang Syne." No offense to Robert Burns, but I bet when he wrote the famous poem back in 1788 he wasn't planning on folks around the world holding hands at midnight and singing it hundreds of years later.

Usually when I'm singing it with a group, it sort of sounds like "Should old acquaintance be forgot and naaaaaa, na-na na naaaaaa . . . Should naaaaa, na-na na, naaaaaaa na na an-nd ollllllld lang's eyes."

Until we get a new song, our only solution is actually knowing more than three words of the one we've got. Here, lemme do us both a favor and print them here for a cheat sheet. Just a few extra words will keep it going.

Pull out this book on New Year's and kick it off on a high note. AWESOME!

CHEAT SHEET!

Should old acquaintance be forgot,
and never brought to mind?
Should old acquaintance be forgot,
and old lang syne?

CHORUS:

For auld lang syne, my dear,
for auld lang syne,
we'll take a cup of kindness yet,
for auld lang syne.

And surely you'll buy your pint cup!
and surely I'll buy mine!
And we'll take a cup o' kindness yet,
for auld lang syne.

CHORUS

We two have run about the slopes,
and picked the daisies fine;
But we've wandered many a weary foot,
since auld lang syne.

CHORUS

We two have paddled in the stream,
from morning sun till dine;
But seas between us broad have roared
since auld lang syne.

CHORUS

And there's a hand my trusty friend!
And give us a hand o' thine!
And we'll take a right good-will draught,
for auld lang syne.

CHORUS

The last ten seconds of the year

....

Ten!

   Nine!

      Eight!

         Seven!

            Six!

               Five!

                  Four!

                     Three!

                        Two!

                           One!

                              AWESOME!

Staying up so late that everything becomes funny

....

Midnight is long gone.

You hid out in the basement during the grown-up party, you squeezed **sleeping bags together** with high school pals after the ball dropped, or you crash-landed on the corduroy couch with your college roommates when the bar finally said, "Happy New Year! Now go home."

Either way, it's time to face facts: **You're up way too late.**

Your eyes burn a bit, **your head spaces out**, random arms or legs start throbbing, and maybe your scalp gets really, really, really, really itchy. Point is, you've ignored your body's **Go to Sleep** signals for hours, so now you're hunched over a walking stick, squinting deep into the foggy darkness of four, five, six in the morning.

The good news is your brain has developed just the system to charge you up with extra juice and help you power through. Yes, we're talking about massively lowered **Standards of Hilarity**, which help make everything funny. Someone steps on a Styrofoam plate of chip crumbs or kicks a can of Coke onto the carpet, and suddenly everyone looks up at one another with tired raccoon eyes and . . . just starts cracking up.

Late night laughing on New Year's Eve is a beautiful moment because we're getting giggles in with good friends. Shot glasses at the bar lie empty, chip bowls are smeared with grease and crumbs, and sleeping bags or pullouts get wheeled into the scene. All differences dissolve when we realize we're all part of the same **Bleary-eyed Cackling** clan— telling bad jokes, laughing till it hurts, and smiling till sunrise.

AWESOME!

Not getting a hangover when you were expecting to get one

....

Don't ask me how this happens. Sometimes it just happens. AWESOME!

Catching someone you love admiring you from across the room

....

Baby, it's true.

Toss your mushy clump of skin, blood, and bones together and we get the beautifully strange and wonderful package that combines to form *you*. Jokes and smarts, **stutters and starts**, smiles and farts—we're into your everything even though we probably don't tell you enough.

But that's why it's a beautiful moment when you glance up from the **party chatter or kitchen clatter** and catch your valentine smiling silently at you from across the room.

Maybe it's the dog head-tilting from the couch as you race to grab your keys and run out the door all stressed, **maybe it's your daughter sneaking a peek in the bathroom mirror as you zip up your dress**, or maybe it's your grandma smiling with wet eyes as you stick your hands in the cake and make a mess.

Maybe it's your little brother smiling from the stands as you come up to home plate, **maybe it's your mom waiting at the train station for you to come through the gate**, or maybe it's your boyfriend staring at the **back of the bus** at the end of your Valentine's Day date.

When you catch those quick and quiet glances, let your heart melt and feel at peace, because you just got told without words that you are admired, you are treasured, and **you are loved**.

Happy Valentine's Day.

AWESOME!

When your third grade arch nemesis gives you a Valentine's Day card

....

D id your school have a social ladder?

My school sure did, and I was sitting pretty on the bottom rung, people. How could I tell? Well, for one thing, I was always picked last for dodgeball in gym class. For some reason, my **giant glasses** and tiny, spaghetti-noodle arms didn't inspire the jocks, and they usually took the boy in the wheelchair and the girl with crutches before me. Social status was also on display on the bus—from back to front, from jock to runt, it was a **Pyramid of Cool** bouncing home from school every day.

But above all! More than anything! Our social ladder was on display for the great big moment on Valentine's Day. Yes, long before the **One Card for All** communist classroom manifesto was enacted, it was all about how many cards you collected on February 14th. That was when Kleenex boxes were tissue-papered with pink hearts and transformed into delightfully tacky mailboxes hanging from the side of your desk.

Everyone wore **red, white, and pink** to school, the teacher brought cupcakes, and soon it was time for the great big moment of racing around the room to drop your paper valentines into people's paper boxes.

You could count on getting valentines from a few close friends, but everyone else was a crapshoot. Some people would bring one for everyone. Others forgot completely. And sometimes you'd score a surprise valentine from your third grade arch nemesis that made it all worth it.

When the kid who shoves you in the mud at recess asks you to be his forever . . . well, that's a tiny little moment of

AWESOME!

Getting a dinner reservation even though you waited till the last minute

....

Y ou had big ideas.

There was the romantic horse ride through the park at dusk followed by a **candlelit dinner** at the Italian place with checkered tablecloths. Then there was the hand-holding vision you had of smiling in the quiet corner of the stuffy French restaurant while sharing a bottle of champagne and getting **two spoons** for creme brulee. Then there was just scoring a booth at the Mexican chain for greasy fajitas and lots of sour cream.

Then there was just getting any reservation anywhere.

Let's be honest—despite your best intentions to make a reservation a few weeks ago, you somehow just didn't pull it off. You meant to, **you really meant to**, but now you're stuck sweating and scrambling.

So you call and you call and you call and you call and you call and then suddenly! Without warning! The new downtown restaurant you've both been dying to try has a cancellation!

And they can fit you in! And you're smiling, and you're excited, and you feel a massive wave of relief suddenly wash over you.

And she never ever needs to know.

AWESOME!

Getting homemade coupons for foot massages and favorite dinners

S crew Hallmark.

Those money-squeezing punks have been raking coin for years off our inability to talk about our emotions. I'm saying these **landfill-stuffing fat cats** won't get their comeuppance until their five-dollar pieces of pink paper are gone, gone, gone like the wind.

Because seriously, folks: Homemade greeting cards just do the job much better. Writing from the heart, **lipstick-kissing the sheet**, or just saying "I Love You" with a couple colored markers goes so much further than the cursive stylings on the drugstore shelf.

Truly, the only thing that can improve the **Homemade Greeting Card Experience** is when a couple homemade coupons

fall out of it. Yes, scoring "1 free foot massage" or "Your favorite meal, cooked by me" really sweetens the deal and gets the
whole night glowing with love.

Plus you just saved five bucks.

AWESOME!

Hearing someone's heartbeat

Y ou had a great day.

You traded sexy texts in the morning, got a home-made greeting card, and found flowers waiting at home.

Now you're lying on the grass, lazing on the couch, or relaxing in some crumpled sheets, and you just **fall into the moment** with the person you love. After the conversation dies down and the background noise fades away, you smile silently and melt into an **arms-and-legs embrace**. Gaze into their eyes, push your ears to their chest, and then shhhhhhhhhhhhhhhh.

Just listen.

AWESOME!

Not getting extra-small lingerie as a present

O h, the relief!
    Love may be blind, but ladies don't always like testing that theory out while wearing dental floss as underwear.
    AWESOME!

Being single and just enjoying it

··

e see you, we hear you.

We see those movie endings and we hear those greeting cards. We know the cheesy quotes and we sing those ballads at bars. We feel those **preaching choirs** and we read those magazine tips. We feel our parents pushing and we hear your chatty lips.

Yes, we know having a boyfriend is great and we know it's beautiful and kind. But all we're saying today, and all we're trying to prove, is that you don't need a killer girlfriend to have a killer mood.

Valentine, let's chat about ten winning ways to celebrate your solo days:

1. **Some like it hot.** When you're on your own you're the master of the tank, and the chances of a random flush scalding your skin are pretty slim. You're less likely to run out of hot water, so just twist that dial and soak into the zone.

2. **One set of parents.** Sure, you lose out on some In-law Naps, but you could gain back holiday budgets,

extra bedrooms, and Saturday evenings. (Note to any in-laws reading this: This entry is about other in-laws, not you.)

3. **Take back the night.** When you're bumping around by yourself, there's no need to worry about making too much noise early or late. Tiptoes, quiet TV watching, and softly shutting doors take a backseat to cranking tunes, late night phone calls, and your big galoomping feet.

4. **Don't be an ass.** Single folks have no obligation to do joint Halloween costumes like Beauty and the Beast or the classic two-person donkey. Because don't we all feel a little bit sorry for that couple dressed as salt and pepper shakers leaving the party at 10 pm?

5. **Flirt like you mean it.** Chitchatting with sparkly objects of your desire is good fun. When you're single, ditch the guilt and holler at the busty waitress or chiseled cop. Not only is it exciting, but you're building your social side and meeting new people.

6. **Getting to know you.** You're the only you you've got. Born and blasted into the world, you're a baby brain who flies through life forming crackly connections with everyone you meet. But getting to know yourself through experiences and inner thoughts adds

important shapes and smears to your awareness and identity.

7. **Bargain basement holidays.** Tap your wallet and smile when you walk by that towering display of heart-filled chocolates and pink teddy bears.

8. **You can get with this or you can get with that.** Are you hungry at 11 pm? Get a burger! Are you bored on a Saturday night? Hit the scene! Do you want to free up your busy weekend or busy up your free one? Well, the choice is yours! You can get with this or you can get with that. I think you'll get with this for this is where it's at.

9. **Own your bed, own your life.** When you're single the entire bed is yours and you can test a variety of starfish poses, Chun-Li leg-kick positions, or even the extremely bold diagonal sleeping (rarely done).

10. **Embrace your disgusting habits.** Clipping your toenails in bed, napping in piles of dirty clothes, or chomping greasy handfuls of potato chips over the sink is fine, fine, fine. The mirror won't judge you and neither will anybody else.

So, people, let's hear it for being single if you're single this Valentine's Day.

Exploring the world, finding adventures, and scoping big

scenes are hallmarks of being cool with being you. Because look—falling in love is great and falling in love is nice, but that doesn't mean going solo can't also be sugar and spice. Good days and bad days, **setting suns and shining stars**, it's all about perspective and focusing on who you are. Because if all you need is love, and all love needs is you, then it's great to relax and enjoy . . . just being you with you.

AWESOME!

Claiming that you're
an eighth Irish

....

We don't all have red hair and freckles.

But if you get a couple pints of Guinness in us, we're gonna chat your ear off about how if you go back far enough on our mom's side there was this one great-aunt who was actually born just outside of Dublin.

AWESOME!

Your friend's horrible Irish accent

....

It's your buddy at the office wishing a **"Top o' the morning to ye!"** when you get to work. It's your girlfriend wearing a plastic green hat and ordering a Guinness with a "wee coaster to place it on." It's your college pal walking beside you on the way home ranting about how U2, Lucky Charms, and potatoes are underrated.

Yes, there's just something hilarious about hearing a friend tell a story with a **horrible Irish accent**. If you're lucky, the terrible impersonation becomes a new joke itself and you end up laughing in a never-ending cycle of

AWESOME!

When Shamrock Shakes suddenly appear at McDonald's

....

Who remembers McDonaldland?

Yes, it was that trippy make-believe world where all the McDonald's characters lived in harmony. Growing up, we occasionally holed up in the corner of McDonald's when someone's **cool mom** dropped some bills on a deliciously greasy birthday party. There was usually **a giant mural** along the wall with all the McDonaldland characters living fantasy lives in their all-burgers-all-the-time world. If you were lucky, you might even have played on the McDonaldland playground equipment with some of these guys.

Now everyone knows the standard characters of **the Hamburglar**, who was dressed in black-and-white-striped prison garb so we knew he just broke out of the slammer. I always figured he'd gotten sick of tuna melts and grilled cheeses and just had to have his fix. And there was **Mayor McCheese**, who despite his giant wobbly cheeseburger head was really as suave as they come. After all, he wore a top hat, diplomat's sash, and fancy reading specs, and I assumed he always stopped by the opera after leaving city hall. And let's not forget everyone's favorite, **Grimace**, who played the lovable purple doofus of some as-yet-unknown gender.

But my favorite of the whole bunch was the rarely seen **Uncle O'Grimacey**. Basically, he was Grimace's Irish uncle who visited every March. He looked just like Grimace too! Except he was green instead of purple and he wore a four-leaf clover vest.

I loved Uncle O'Grimacey because his annual visit in the TV commercials meant it was time for **Shamrock Shakes** at McDonald's. These bright green minty milkshakes were always an elusive and delightful break from the other flavors. And slamming back Shamrock Shakes was the childhood equi-

valent of drinking Guinness at the bar. Sure, maybe it wasn't good for us, but somewhere between the dangerous plasti-mold playgrounds and dimly lit corners by the bathroom existed a magical world full of childhood memories, neon green milkshakes, and greasy wrapped packages full of

AWESOME!

Giving up something really easy for Lent

That's it.

No more skydiving.

AWESOME!

When Mom buys the solid chocolate instead of the hollow chocolate

Do you love your kids?

Well, according to *Terrible Parenting* magazine, giving your child a hollow Easter bunny means you don't. Honestly, it ranks up there with obliterating them at Ping-Pong, **stealing their chicken skin,** or making them go to bed while the sun's still out.

Don't be that mom.

Because as much as we enjoy watching bunny's hollow skull crumble into a pile of chocolate crumbs on the kitchen table, the truth is the solid bunny has so many advantages. It lasts about five times as long, **it's more fun to gnaw on,** and it doubles as a weapon against the very sister who tries to steal it.

So come on! Get us a solid bunny this year, Mom.

Then we'll know you're

AWESOME!

Stocking up on clearance chocolate the week after Easter

....

It's like panning for gold.

Bundle up and head north to your local Megamart before combing shelves with patience and care. Windy days, **cold nights**, and a diligent work ethic should be rewarded with finding that hidden patch of clearance candy at the back of the store.

Time to load your cart with solid bunnies, little mesh bags of chocolate eggs, and anything filled to the gills with creme.

Nothing tastes as good as a deal.

AWESOME!

Finding a hidden chocolate egg way after Easter

Surprise!

While mindlessly dragging your hand between the couch cushions, **sweeping the backyard patio stones**, or searching for extra batteries in the junk drawer, a tiny foiled egg suddenly appears like a sugary gift from the heavens.

And when you score that surprise chocolate dropping, just remember there can be absolutely no stopping before **quick-peeling and quick-popping** that chocolate straight into your mouth. Time of day, hunger level, age of chocolate—none of this matters. Frankly, if you're stuffed on breakfast pancakes and the chocolate is powdery white and tastes like foil from two Easters ago . . . that is victory.

Yes, finding a chocolate egg way after Easter is an eyes-wide moment of taste-based wonder.

Finding a chocolate egg way after Easter is

AWESOME!

Getting served
breakfast in bed

....

Happy Mother's Day!

It's 7:30 am and your kids wake you up with a plate of cold toast, runny eggs, and a short glass of **lukewarm OJ**. Sure, it may not be the best-tasting meal in the world, and yeah, you might fill your sheets with crumbs, but don't tell me getting served breakfast isn't the greatest.

I mean, there you were just sleeping there. And someone else said, "Let's go downstairs and cook up our best possible meal, toss it on a tray, and bring it upstairs and serve it to you." Yes, serve it to you! Cook it up and set it up and serve it to you. I have to say you're pretty lucky if this happens to you.

Plus, breakfast in bed can also help accomplish the exotic **get up and eat up and get back down** move, a brilliant Saturday or Sunday feat that involves filling your belly with breakfast and then immediately crashing back into a **post-fiesta siesta**. Yes, it's a great feeling to go back to bed with that full stomach. And who knows? Maybe there's a **lunch in bed** just waiting for you on the other side of those sleepy dreams. But really, it's a good question—has anyone ever actually scored **lunch** in bed? If so, I'm pretty sure they win the **World's Greatest Mother's Day Ever** contest.

Now, the Trump Card for turning a good breakfast in bed into a great one is when it includes one or more of the following:

- One of those tiny, miniature glass bottles of ketchup or jam
- A homemade greeting card wishing you a Happy Mother's Day or Happy Birthday
- A breakfast dessert of any kind
- Butter painstakingly carved into a perfect sphere
- Cute, restaurant-style folded-up napkins

Because let's be honest, people. We sure do love eating. **We sure do love sleeping.** And breakfast in bed is the closest we get to combining both at the same time. And around here, you know what we think of that.

Say it with me now.

AWESOME!

Cool moms

....

I love cool moms.

When I was growing up there was a **Sunny D commercial** on TV where a gang of kids in backward caps and **jammer shorts** roller-skates home before helping Mom bring in the groceries. When they go inside they search between a fridge packed with cola and purple stuff before pulling out a jug of Sunny D to big cheers. Later they're chilling under a tree when Mom returns with an armload of Sunny D. As the scene closes one of the kids screams out, **"You got a cool mom!"**

And despite the **cheesy cheese quality** of this old commercial, there really is something sweet about finding out your friend has a cool mom. Cool moms are often found upstairs at that one house everyone always hangs out at displaying some of these familiar characteristics:

- **Anywhere, anytime sugar.** Cool moms have candy and sugary cereals you don't have at your house, and they've got no problem filling your bowl with Corn Pops after a sleepover or letting you drink a big cup of Coke with dinner.

- **Grease runs for fun.** Loud cheers from the back of the station wagon and the Minivan Applause-O-Meter guide cool moms to ice cream shops and McDonald's drive-thrus. Six-year-olds on soccer teams get sundaes or chip truck fries whenever cool mom is driving them home.

- **Steady behind the wheel.** Cool moms drive your friends all over the place. She's your taxi to the mall food court, baseball diamond, or movie theater. Cool moms also take care not to embarrass you in front of your friends by controlling the bad jokes and goodbye kisses. Sometimes they slip you an extra fiver too.

- **Lax sleepover policies.** She knows you and your teenage friends will watch the R-rated movie in the basement anyway, so cool mom doesn't fuss much with the ratings or the extra half hour of TV before bed. Let the kids talk a bit during the sleepover, she figures. Nobody's getting hurt.

- **Anonymous phone-a-friend always open.** Cool moms give off sparkly vibes of open-mindedness that let kids know their questions won't be judged. Cool moms help draft the apology letter, call the neighbor after tossing a ball through their window, and are always around to chat about anything serious.

When you have a friend with a **cool mom**, you're loving it lots. And if you're a cool mom, your house is full of big smiles, **loud laughs**, and happy kids. You value the best things in life and **live to love** for years and years and years.

Hey, cool moms! Guess what? You're
AWESOME!

Your mom's love

My mom was born in Nairobi, Kenya in 1950.
Growing up the youngest of **eight kids** in a small house off the downtown hub, she was quiet, shy, and always the baby. Her three older brothers received the bulk of the family's praise, attention, and money for education, while the girls were taught to sweep floors, **work the stove**, and scrub the work clothes clean.

My mom used to sit on her front porch and memorize all the **license plates** of cars that drove by. She'd **guess the numbers from a distance**, silently congratulating herself when she got one right. Quiet nights in the corner of the clattery kitchen, she'd study math under dim lights and curious gazes.

In 1963, she took the government's standard National Exam with every other thirteen-year-old in the country. And she aced it.

Suddenly a **fat scholarship** dropped on her and she was whisked off to a preppy English boarding school in the countryside. The next few years were full of reciting **the Lord's Prayer**, memorizing Shakespeare passages, and eating soft-boiled eggs in the corner of the school cafeteria.

After hitting the books hard away from friends and family,

she graduated and started **correspondence classes** from an accounting institution in England, eventually earning her letters, moving to London, and auditing the books of big companies. It was there she met my dad while he was visiting from Canada, and it was there that **they got married** before moving to a small, dusty suburb an hour east of Toronto.

She got a job at **General Motors**, saw her first dentist, ate her first hamburger, and signed up for a subscription to *Reader's Digest*. When I was growing up, she'd tell me her coworkers always asked what she was doing there. "Let me get this straight," they'd begin. "You lived in Nairobi. You lived in London. How'd you end up in this small town?"

But it was in that small town she had my sister and me, and it was in that small town she showered us with love every day since we were born. Although I never knew my grandparents, my mom filled the void with unending praise and patience.

She took me to the library Saturday mornings and helped me slowly finger-read **Hardy Boys** books. She signed my sister and me up for camps and let us quit if we came home crying. When I routinely got pegged first playing dodgeball at **Boy Scouts** or broke my glasses playing soccer, she was always there, ready with a hug and an "It's okay, Neil, it's okay . . . it's okay."

For a good chunk of the past year, I was getting three or

four hours of sleep a night balancing my day job, writing my blog, **1000 Awesome Things**, and working out the stresses of life. Every few weeks over this time, my mom took the commuter train to my downtown apartment with a big canvas bag and loaded up my freezer with homemade food.

And before she left, she'd reach up to give me a big hug and say, "Don't forget to take a break."

So this one goes out to the moms of the world. This one goes out to the people who raised you. I know I wouldn't have made it without that love and support, and I'm sure some of you are in the same place. So, moms, thank you for teaching us to read, **thanks for cheering our dreams**, and thanks for helping us grow up to become a little more

AWESOME!

Getting homemade crafts from your kids

....

Admit it.

You gave your mom some horribly ugly craft when you were a kid. I hope it wasn't as bad as the giant life-sized Play-Doh model of my mom's face I made in seventh grade. Even though it looked a bit like she was a **cross-eyed ogre** wearing a shiny helmet, she told me she loved it and kept it sitting on her dresser for years.

And that's what it's all about.

Whether it's the pipe-cleaner-and-glitter construction paper spelling out *I love you*, the **tiny day-care handprints** with the cheesy poem, or the marker-smeared hat made out of a paper plate, the point is the same.

Somebody little loves you.

AWESOME!

Total control over the remote

. . . .

S orry, kids.

We're watching golf and that's that.

Go play outside.

AWESOME!

·

When someone else
mows the lawn

....

I bought a house a few years back.

Basement apartments, **cramped condos**, and old rooms at my parents' place all suddenly faded into the distance as I finally enjoyed the freedom of owning my own pad.

Of course, the only problem was that I **massively underestimated** the amount of work involved in taking care of the place. Shoveling sidewalks, **vacuuming basements**, and pulling weeds from the garden sounded fun until I was suddenly spending every waking hour doing them.

That lawn was the worst of all.

After pushing a rusty mower across the front and backyards, I was left with dirty brown patches of **dead grass** and blade-resistant dandelions standing fiercely by the fence. Yes, I was slaving away for the worst-looking lawn on the street.

Dads, that's why I'm going out on a limb and saying you're loving it when someone else mows the lawn. Kids, listen up—

Dad will take the golf balls and that new **polka-dot tie** in the morning, but if you really want to get on his good side, you know what to do.

Start the engine and get pushing.

AWESOME!

Actually finding a good present for Dad

W̶e love moms.

They're so easy to buy for! Hit the kitchen store, **stop at the jewelry shop**, and order some flowers. But dads, well—not so much. See, as much as Dad loves polka-dot ties, the truth is that he'd love something a bit more creative.

So I'm going to be honest here.

You need to get your dad a gift basket.

Yes, stuff one full of golf ball sleeves, **universal remote controls**, and power tools.

And suddenly you're the favorite son.

AWESOME!

Big crowds enjoying big fireworks together

. . . .

Fire trickles and drips across the sky, old folks huddle and cuddle and babies cry, teenagers squeeze sweaty palms and look up, up way high. Because light fills the night, **kabooms bang in the air**, conversations stop, jaws drop, we all crane our necks up . . . and stare. Yes, when those fireworks erupt, when they splash in the dark, **when those bright waterfalls drip down into our park**, we all *oooh* and *ahhh* at them big beautiful sparks.

AWESOME!

Catching the ice cream truck

....

Candy doesn't deliver.

Since **Emperor Nero** sent slaves into the mountains for ice to mix with honey and nuts two thousand years ago, we've all enjoyed cooling off with big bowls of the sweet and icy treat.

Yup, Arabs started adding milk to the mixture a thousand years later, the Chinese invented an ice cream maker, and our friends in France were first to write it down in a cookbook. Basically, everybody around **Team Planet** contributed to the unparalleled levels of creamy deliciosity we all enjoy today.

Nowadays maybe you get your fix when the soccer team screams at Mom from the back of the station wagon till she peels into the Dairy Queen parking lot. Or maybe you sneak down to the basement freezer for a few sneaky spoonfuls after bedtime.

Or maybe you actually catch a truck on the Fourth of July.

You know how it goes.

Scribbling on your stomach in your bedroom, playing **Bubble Bobble** with your brother in the basement, throwing baseballs with your dad in the backyard, your ears suddenly perk up to the sound of a distant and familiar jingling. And for once those bells ringing don't mean classes about to start at school.

Eyeballs pop, **eyebrows raise**, and big smiles curl on your face, because now the race is on.

Booming down the hall, bouncing down the stairs, you scramble for spare change as those jingling bells get louder and louder and **louder**. Forget socks, forget shoes, forget closing the front door—it's time to blast out of the house and risk the **Burning Blackfoot** as you sprint as fast as you can down the street toward that slow-wheeling, rainbow-colored truck . . .

. . . and once you score your **sweet and creamy plunder**, it's time to get licking before diving into a hot dog and coleslaw dinner and heading to the park for the fireworks show.

Can't you just taste it?

AWESOME!

Really, really selling it while barbecuing

....

That thick, smoky **barbecue smell** floats through the yard and everybody starts salivating for dinner.

Yes, sizzling sides of beef and burnt-black wieners are coming right up when the sun's dropping, **the party's hopping,** and your friends are all chilling with ice-cracking drinks on your backyard patio. And if you're in charge of grilling up dinner, then there aren't many things that scream **I'm Serious About This** more than really, really selling it to all your friends. Oh sure, some things come close, such as:

- owning a shiny, oversized nine-piece barbecue tool set and having it folded open on the picnic table.

- not leaving the barbecue at any point and even holding on to the handle when the lid is down to make sure nobody attempts to flip burgers when you aren't looking.

- wearing a giant apron with your name on it.

- asking everybody constant questions at all times, such as "Did you say medium or medium-well?"

and "You're toasted, you're toasted, you're un-toasted, right?"

Yeah, don't get me wrong, all those things shout **I'm Serious About This**, too. But nothing quite screams it like **really, really selling it to the crowd.** You know what I'm talking about if you've ever hammed it up with any of these classic moves:

- "Dog up, I gotta dog up, who wants a dog?!"
- "Come on, Andrew, you're not eating salad, are you? Come on, how many more can I sign you up for? Two at least?"
- (Walking around the deck with raised eyebrows, holding a cold cheeseburger on your BBQ flipper, and occasionally waggling it in someone's face.)
- "Okay, I got a slightly burnt one. Who likes them nice and crispy? Nice and crispy one here, every-body. Niiiiice and crispy."

Yes, if you're getting your **barbecue groove** on strong and you're **rocking the sales pitch** long, then kudos to you. Every deck party needs somebody to tell everybody else to eat more hamburgers. So today we salute you for embracing the job. You sold it. **We bought it.** And now we're all feeling stuffed, bloated, and completely

AWESOME!

Driving around with the windows down on late summer nights

....

K ids cruise on wobbly bikes, **toddlers race on tipsy trikes,** and you drift deep into the hot summer night. Swerve and curve on windy roads as darkness slowly falls and **stars pop out** to reveal a twinkly twilight glow. As you hit the gas and drop your windows the warm beating rush of summer air makes you smile and makes everything else in the world just fade away . . . fade away . . . fade away . . . fade away . . . f

AWESOME!

The moment on a road trip when you're really far from where you started and really far from where you're going

Do you know that **rickety bridge scene** from the movies? Violins screech and kettle drums swell as our hero tiptoes across a dangerous rope bridge swinging wildly over a dark canyon at the pulsing climax of the film. The audience gasps and grips their armrests as she **kicks a loose plank** and the camera painfully watches it whip and shatter against the rocky cliffside before falling into the deep river rapids below.

But after some tense moments, there's a beautiful wide shot of our hero stepping slowly past the **saggy midpoint** of that flimsy bridge . . . and that's when she first commits to going all the way. Turning back isn't a shortcut anymore, turning back isn't an option, and so she firms those lips, **steadies those hips**, and plows forward with steely-eyed determination till she gets to the other side.

Scenes like that remind me of hitting that beautiful **middle-of-nowhere midpoint** on a summer road trip. After you packed your bags, coolers, and kids, you had the guts to zoom out of your neighborhood in the middle of the heat. Now you're a highway explorer whipping past barns and water towers, **twiddling onto distant radio stations**, and staring up at a whole new world just a few feet away . . .

AWESOME!

Boat waving

....

If you're lucky, your summer holidays can include cottage time, **beach vacations**, or sailing way out into the ocean.

And when you're out on the water, don't forget the rules of the sea.

If you're on a boat **you must wave** to anyone who waves at you from another boat, **you must wave** to anyone who waves at you from land, and **you must initiate waving** to as many other boats as possible.

The only way you can avoid these rules is if you're a dog, or a pirate, or both.

AWESOME!

Watching the Christmas episode of your favorite sitcom in the completely wrong month

....

Thank you for being a friend.

When you're crashing into the couch in the cold basement and flicking on the **TV screen**, there's nothing as nice as being surrounded by your favorite pals in familiar places. Yes, there really is something great about bumping into the Christmas special in the completely wrong time of the year.

Whether Kevin's got to find a Christmas gift for Winnie, George battles his Festivus demons, or the Tanner family gets stranded at the airport on Christmas Eve, well . . . it's a sprinkle of Christmas spirit in the middle of your July.

Those Christmas specials usually feature the full cast of characters, **surprise music interludes**, and huggy closing scenes that zoom out to snowflakes falling past frosty windows and flickering red lights strung across rooftops. Christmas episodes remind us where we were when we first saw them and give us a surprise dose of holiday family values right when we least expect it.

Christmas episode, your heart is true.

You're a pal and a confidant.

AWESOME!

Digging out your own little wading pool in the sand when you're at the beach

···

L ife begins with climate control.

Since we first hung woolly mammoth furs from forest branches, we've gotten used to getting comfy when we settle in somewhere. Just look at babies in those curly fetal poses in their flannel onesies, look at them napping in sun hats and shades in strollers, look at them cuddling up to Mom in cozy carry-ons.

Folks, it's like I always say: **We can learn much from The Baby.**

Digging out your own little wading pool in the sand when you're at the beach is another beautiful moment of climate control. You strip down because you're hot, take a dip to cool off, chill out in the sand . . . and are suddenly hot again. Now it's time to get digging and fill your in-ground **Sand Chair** with water to cool off those nether regions so you can relax and have it both ways.

AWESOME!

Skinny-dipping somewhere you shouldn't be

··

Y ou were meant to be naked.

After swimming in a stomach, you came out crying in a new world full of harsh lights, **surgical masks**, and cold tables. A couple minutes later you were quickly covered in plastic, wool, and cotton, but you never forgot.

You never forgot.

Yes, you've been in clothes for years, you've been in clothes since that day, you've been wearing socks forever, you've been wearing shoes the same way.

But . . . sometimes pants are a pain and shirts are a mess and life's just a lot better when you're completely undressed.

You were meant to be naked.

You came here without clothes.

You were meant to be naked.

And sometimes you gotta go back to what you know.

Stripping in the hot tub, **jumping off the dock**, slipping your swimming trunks off, and showing the world your . . . confidence.

Yes, I say just be out there and be happy, be out there and rewind, just get naked and relax, get naked . . . and forget time.

AWESOME!

Lighting firecrackers
and eating greasy foods
with your family

H ow's your Diwali education?

Forgive me, but mine needs brushing up, so here
goes.

Diwali is a five-day festival of lights that includes spicing
up your pad with lamps and candles, **lighting firecrackers**, eating treats and sweets, and trading gifts during some serious
family time.

Hindus, Sikhs, Jains, and anyone who loves a good party
all enjoy the festival in October or November, depending on
when it lines up with the Hindu calendar. Although it's most
commonly celebrated in South Asian communities, like most
parties that have been raging for thousands of years it's pop-
ular all over our spinning rock.

See, a guy named Valmiki wrote an epic poem almost
three thousand years ago called *Ramayana*, which forms the
basis of the holiday. Oh, and by the way, this epic poem is **truly**
epic—the entire thing is 27,000 verses and fills up seven
books! I'm not sure, but I think if you read it all you get your

face up on the wall of the library and a mesh hat reading "I can't believe I read the whole thing."

In the story, the main character Lord Rama is sent to live in the forest for fourteen years by his father. But everyone loved Rama so they waited the fourteen years out, while he hung out with his brother, Lakshmana, and his wife, Sita. It was kind of a **slumber party under the stars** until the evil demon king Ravana kidnapped Sita and stole her away to an island. Thankfully, Rama had a little help from his friends like big Hanuman, and he eventually managed to defeat Ravana and return home.

So Diwali is the festival of lights that commemorates Lord Rama's return. To celebrate his defeat of Ravana, the townspeople burst firecrackers, lit up houses, and decked out the entire city in lights to help him find his way.

These days Diwali is marked by the same lights, which serve to represent the victory of good over evil within every person. Yes, it's time to get together with friends and family, **stuff your face with samosas**, and enjoy a big rowdy day full of AWESOME!

Hilarious last-minute Halloween costumes

. . . .

Back at college, I remember walking up to my friend Mike's house on Halloween and seeing him frantically painting **bright red briefs** onto a pair of nice blue jeans. He was really going at it, too—slapping the wet brush all over the crotch and pockets, wagging his tongue out like a dog.

Of course, an hour later he showed up to the party as Superman. And though he didn't leap any tall buildings in a single bound, he did manage to drink most of the punch bowl faster than a speeding bullet.

More important, his last-minute Halloween costume got us all laughing. Some of the best ones do that.

- **Professional baseball player.** This is where you dig through your closet and peel out that old sweat-smelling jersey and orange foam hat from Little League. Throw on your baseball glove and paint some thick black lines under your eyes and you're good to go.

- **Sandwich.** My friend Brian once slapped a piece of bread on his chest and another on his back and went as a sandwich. You've heard of a Quarter Pounder, right? Well, this was a two-hundred pounder.

- **Vending machine.** Here's where you duct-tape little bags of chips and chocolate bars all over your body. If your party's working properly, they'll be ripped off you within ten minutes of getting there.

- **The random closet mish-mash with a funny name.** You've got a purple tie, dark shades, and leather pants, so you go as a Club-Going Comedian With A Black Eye. You've got a bridesmaid dress, oven mitts, and a tiara, so you go as Lounge Singer Baking Cookies For A Bachelorette Party. You get the idea.

- **Jabba the Hutt.** Time to laze around on the couch in a green sleeping bag.

- **The Walk of Shame.** Simply wear a man's shirt over your dress clothes, mess up your hair, and hold a pair of high heels in your hand. For guys, try a backward, inside-out shirt, sideways bedhead, and your shoes on the wrong feet.

- **A Terrible Record Collection.** My friend Alec once bought a milk crate of old records for a quarter from a garage sale. They were in horrible condition, but the price was right, so he took them home. For Halloween, he safety-pinned most of them on himself and went as A Terrible Record Collection. It was a good laugh, but since he couldn't really move, he ended up spending most of the party whisper-singing "Monster Mash" to himself on a futon.
- **Grapes.** Boy, if you've got some purple or green balloons lying around, have we got a costume for you.
- **Yourself.** This is where you arrive at the party completely unprepared, but rather than fess up you just tell people you're going as yourself this year. Then whenever someone says, "But that's not a costume," you say, "Maybe it is . . ." and give them a really exaggerated wink.

Okay listen, when somebody puts an amazing amount of time and effort into a **kick-ass costume**, that's worth celebrating. Nobody here denies that. All we're saying today is if you manage to scramble around your house at the last minute and get us all laughing with your hilariously creative costume, then that's completely admirable.

It's simply commendable.

It's downright respectable.

And we all know it's just totally

AWESOME!

That one house on your street that gets really, really into Halloween

....

What level are you?

Level 0. Real cobwebs, one pumpkin lying on the porch that isn't carved, lollipops in a popcorn bowl.

Level 1. Fake stringy cobwebs across the front door, carved jack-o'-lantern lying on the porch, plastic Halloween-themed sign on the door, mini candy bars handed out of a giant plastic orange pumpkin.

Level 2. Fake stringy cobwebs everywhere with giant black plastic spiders on them, more than two jack-o'-lanterns on the porch with real candles flickering inside, creepy music of creaky doors and rattling chains playing through the window, candy handed out by someone wearing a *Scream* mask or long black cape, a pretend dead guy in a patio chair on the porch who turns out to be real when you get close to him.

Level 3. Garage transformed into haunted house featuring actual black cat, more than three jack-o'-lanterns carved into detailed works of art, orange and black lightbulbs up the walk, full candy bars handed out by Halloween philanthropists in makeup and costumes, entire lawn transformed into graveyard with cardboard gravestones reading things like "Here lies good ol' Colorblind Fred, thought the lights were green when they were red," a pretend dead guy in a patio chair who actually turns out to be pretend because there's another guy hiding in the bushes behind you who actually scares you, fog machine.

AWESOME!

Strategic trick-or-treating

Trick-or-treating ain't no game.

No, it's a life lesson in goal-setting, planning, and tactical execution. Kids who master trick-or-treating go on to become successful world leaders. Kids who don't could possibly also do the same, but with less chocolate to show for it. The point is that chocolate is delicious, and you should fill your pillowcase with as much of it as possible. You just have to master the **Five Rules of Strategic Trick-or-Treating** first:

5. **Mo' money, mo' problems.** In terms of **where** to go trick-or-treating, there's always a lot of chatter about getting a ride over to the rich neighborhood for the big score. People would have you believe that the rich enjoy lavishing children with unopened boxes of Twinkies and full cases of root beer. But that's a lie! Rich people got rich by being cheap, and their massive front yards will just slow you down. That's right, you'll be navigating wrought-iron fences, duck-shaped hedges, and koi ponds instead of ringing doorbells. Instead, aim

for the new neighborhood with little kids and the all-important densely packed homes.

4. **Bag the bag.** If you're lugging around a hard neon orange jack-o'-lantern, then you're dead before you've even gone around the street. Nope, you need to go for volume, durability, and handles. Some people swear by the pillowcase, but what you gain in volume you lose in convenience. Wrist cramps and Santa Claus–like sack-lugging are no way to run up and down the block. Go for a sturdy bag that can withstand being tossed over a fence or wrestled away from a dog.

3. **Dress for success.** Trick-or-treating is a race against the clock, so set yourself up for success by wearing running shoes and avoiding masks that affect your visibility. No ballet slippers, high heels, or sandals. No robes, capes, or togas. And none of those cheap plastic masks from the dollar store that attach with a thin elastic and a couple of staples. Basically, keep simplifying your costume and then timing yourself running up and down the basement stairs until you've found a winner. If in doubt, go as Carl Lewis.

2. **Partner up.** It will be tempting to form a trick-or-treating posse and move from door to door as one

big, shifty amoeba of fluorescent tape and face paint. **Resist that temptation.** The amoeba will cause two problems: First, the group will travel at the speed of the slowest member. That means one kid with flat feet and asthma ruins everyone's night. Secondly, a big group triggers the rationing instinct in the person handing out candy. They become overwhelmed and default to the "One for you, one for *you*" candy-for-everyone technique. You don't want that. So instead, you need to pick one partner. Qualifications for that lucky someone include a low resting heart rate, winning smile, and really cute costume. The last one is key. The costume must trigger the "Aren't you adorable!" reflex, which inspires extra candy. The gold standard here is a fit toddler in a ladybug costume with new Reeboks.

1. **Timing is everything.** The last rule is all about the three key stages of Halloween candy collecting. Times may vary depending where you're from, but they go something like this:

- **The 4–6 pm Start-up:** You must be very active and running around here, before the street gets too busy. This is your time to hit the houses at the peak of their inventory levels, when they may hand out more because of excess supply or poor foresight.

- **The 6–7 pm Rest Up:** This is when the streets are their busiest. Don't get caught in other people's amoebas. Now's the time to go home and dump out the bag and refresh the face paint. Also, it's a good time to hit your local fast-food joints. McDonald's is usually pretty generous.

- **The 7–9 pm Cleanup:** Now it's all about picking up the scraps. Some houses will be left with too much candy and they'll start giving handfuls instead of fingerfuls. Others will feel guilty about running out and start handing out creative treats from their kitchen, like cups of pudding or boxes of Jell-O powder. The Cleanup stage is a real test of your cardio fitness levels, as many houses will have turned out their lights by now, forcing you to zigzag the street in search of the remaining bounty.

Now that you've got a game plan, just remember to keep it clean out there. Under cover of night and camouflage face paint, some folks venture into the murky trick-or-treating ethical gray zone. Stay away from these folks, because while they're telling people it's their birthday too, collecting a second bag for a "sick sibling at home," or bodychecking toddlers into bushes on their way up the walk, you can rest knowing that you came out to play by the rules.

And you won.

AWESOME!

Intense post-Halloween candy trades

....

$\mathbf{Y}$ou came, **you dressed up**, you conquered.

Now you're walking around with bloodshot eyes and a **gumball headache** as you pack princess costumes into boxes, peel decorations off the door, and get ready for the important business of sorting through your loot.

Yes, it is time for you to focus. **FOCUS.** Work through that Halloween hangover and steady your nerves, because it's time to strike some big deals. Maybe a candy currency system even emerges amongst all your siblings and friends.

Large size chocolate bar: 20 points

Loot bag full of assorted treats: $+/-$ 15 points depending on size of bag

Fun-size chips or Doritos: 10 points

Homemade popcorn ball: 6 points

Reese's Peanut Butter Cup: 5 points (especially valuable if special Halloween version)

All other mini candy bars: 4 points

Little pack of fuzzy peaches or sour gummies: 4 points

Cake items such as Twinkies: 3 points

Two-pack of rock-hard gum: 2 points

Licorice: 2 points

Caramels from a big well-known caramel company:
2 points

Lollipops: 2 points (Note: Possible points premium
for large sizes or rare rainbow-colored lollipops.)

Lollipops with chewy stuff in the middle: Either 1 point
or −2 points, depending on whether you have
braces

**Caramels in clear plastic wrap that are overly sticky
and have no name on them and taste like burnt
sugar:** 1 point

Tootsie Rolls: 1 point

Lemon-flavored anything: 0 points

Pen from guy who sells real estate: 0 points

Anything healthy, including raisins or apples: 0 points

**Weird chewy generic Halloween candy with burning
aftertaste:** −1 point.

So pour out your pillowcase and get ready for some **high
stakes deals** on the basement floor. Don't forget to keep your
personal favorites a secret or you'll pay a fool's ransom. (If you
sacrifice three bags of chips for a Twinkie, you've been had.)

Lastly, know who you're up against—does anyone have **nut allergies** or unhealthy addictions to lime flavoring that you can exploit?

Get in there and get deal-making.

Get in there and get teeth-breaking.

Get in there and get

AWESOME!

Getting the emergency exit row on the airplane when you're heading home

· ·

Have you heard the news?

Apparently, the day before Thanksgiving is the busiest day of the year to travel. Yes, that's when college kids fly home with backpacks full of **dirty undies**, twentysomethings cross coasts to see webcam lovers, and families all come together for our one big chance to say thanks.

Thanks!

Now before it's all **smiles and pumpkin pie**, you really do have to get home first. And if you're flying, you've got to deal with traffic jams, long lines, and packed flights.

My brothers and sisters, I'm gonna tell you straight up: If you're stuck flying, you really don't want to sit next to me on an airplane. Chances are good I'll start drooling on your shoulder, accidentally crank your headset volume, or chat your ear off with boring anecdotes while you attempt to stare dreamily at cloudscapes out the window. Yes, you'll politely nod and smile while I go on for half an hour about my **terrible cell phone plan** or the bloating I've been feeling lately. Honestly, if you end up sitting beside me on a plane, I've got just one thing to say to you.

Sorry.

Nobody can save you now.

See, I've only seen one successful strategy for avoiding the torture that is **My Company**. I took a flight recently where the woman next to me cocooned herself into a sensory deprivation chamber of headphones, blankets, and earplugs as soon as we sat down. She no doubt sensed my impending chat attack and defended against it immediately, even elbow-snagging the armrest for good measure.

Since the two of us happened to be sitting in the **emergency exit row**, I therefore became solely responsible for busting the door open if our plane crash-landed. Yes, the flight attendant coached me on emergency moves and I nodded with steely eyes and firm lips while Snoozy Samantha snored on beside me.

After the plane took off, I sat back in my chair feeling like the hero of the flight. After all, it could all come down to me. Sure, the harsh, unforgiving Andes might crunch our plane, but they would never crunch my spirit.

As modest payment for accepting this critical role, I scored some extra legroom to stretch out and relax. While everyone else had their knees in their laps, I was free to leg around freely, keeping my muscles warm and ready in case the going got tough.

Now, as if all that weren't good enough—the hero status, the legroom, the babes—there's also one more big perk emergency exit row folks get for sitting there.

We get out first.

Yes, when the inflatable slide pops open into the river or the **flashing red lights** shine a smoky path into the fiery forest, we are the emergency exit door kicker-openers . . . running out first . . . **leading the way** . . . saving the day.

AWESOME!

The Kids Table

....

I t gets crowded in the kitchen.

When the whole family comes over for the big feast, suddenly Uncle and Auntie's seating plans get to be pretty tight squeezing. Extra chairs are brought from upstairs and **elbows bump elbows** in these beautifully big turkey and stuffing chow downs.

Sometimes it gets so full that the dinner party gets divided by age. Grown-ups hit The Adult Table to catch up on mortgage rates and family gossip while the kids get banished to The Kids Table.

Yes, The Kids Table is where all the kids eat dinner at holiday family gatherings.

It's generally a rickety card table from the basement pushed beside a **yellow plastic one** from the playroom that ends up turning Grandma's hallway into an eat-in kitchen. Sometimes it's two different heights, sometimes the chairs are broken, and usually the whole thing is covered in a plastic Thanksgiving tablecloth freshly ripped from the dollar store cellophane.

No matter what though, The Kids Table is a great place to find **burps, laughs, and juice spills** at a holiday meal. Everyone's enjoying a warm evening with cousins decked out in their finest cable-knit sweaters, rosy red cheeks, and massive bedhead.

The Kids Table is great for many reasons.

First off, **no parents, no problems**. Nope, they're all baking pies, playing Ping-Pong, or eating twenty feet away. The parenting theory here is that the kids sort of form a group safety net who will likely come screaming if somebody gets hurt, so no need for a pesky watchful eye. So with all adults distracted, rules fly out the window and suddenly elbows lean up on tables, **chewed-up brussel sprouts** get hidden in napkins, and somebody starts eating mashed potatoes with their bare hands.

And no matter how old everybody is, the rule at The Kids Table is that you must act like you're seven. Teenagers who think they're too old for the table quickly start blowing bubbles in their milk, pouring salt in people's drinks, and giggling like mad. Then someone **pops a loud fart** and everyone laughs for ten straight minutes.

Lastly, let's not forget that The Kids Table eats first and sometimes features special items, like lasagna with no onions, **random chopped-up hot dogs**, or real Coke.

People, a lot of good times and great moments happen at The Kids Table. Little ones learn from older siblings and cousins. Childhood bonds and friendships are formed over toys, tears, and **gravy spills**. And for kids, it's good practice for eating with high school pals at the local greasy spoon when someone gets their driver's license or scarfing a hangover breakfast with college roommates at the dining hall.

So thank you, The Kids Table.

For all you do.

AWESOME!

Digging a hole in your mashed potatoes and filling it up with gravy

....

G et your mash on long.

Get your mash on strong.

How great is it that a bunch of **rock-hard brown things** yanked from the dirt can turn into a creamy smooth-n-salty canvas of deliciousness right in the middle of our plates? I'm talking salty lumps, I'm talking tasty bumps, I'm talking mashed potatoes, people.

Mashed potatoes are one of the few foods that achieve that rare **10 out of 10** on sculptability:

- **Lakes and ponds.** The classic. Nobody's bending turkey into teapots or folding broccoli into bathtubs, but we've got no problems carving sloppy potatoes into gravy ponds in no time flat.
- **Broken dams.** Need some gravy on that turkey? No problem—just slice a gully in the side of Lake Gravy and watch the salty brown goodness lay a flash flood on that bird.

- **Retaining walls.** Sorry? What's that? Unruly cran-
  berry sauce is threatening to contaminate your
  stuffing? No problem! Just smear some mashed
  potato paste across your plate like mortar and keep
  all the flavors where they belong.

- **Buried volcano.** When you've got the gravy pond sitting pretty on your plate, it's sometimes fun letting
  it soak in and then quickly flipping the entire struc-
  ture onto itself, completely submerging the gravy
  under a thin sheen of potato. Now you've got a
  starchy chest full of treasure.

And because mashed potatoes offer so much potential, it's
not uncommon to see other creations like **green-bean porcu-
pines** or lumpy Pyramids of Giza in the middle of a mashed
potato plate. There really is no limit to the possibilities, so just
remember to dig for the moment, **sculpt for the memories**, and
build for your life.

AWESOME!

Getting the bigger half
of the wishbone

....

Turkey forensic scientists, **international dream researchers**, and amateur wishologists have assembled a significant stack of well-researched papers mathematically suggesting this actually means nothing.

But we both know it's proof your dreams will come true. AWESOME!

Getting away with putting three desserts on your plate

....

It's time to fill your plate with two kinds of pie, Grandma's homemade squares, a few scattered pieces of fruit, and a big swirl of whipped cream over everything.

Nobody will judge you on Thanksgiving.

Just make sure you use the big plate.

AWESOME!

The Turkey Coma

. . . .

A fter getting stuffed with stuffing and **packed with pota-toes**, someone kindly rolls you to the couch and covers you with old blankets and rogue scraps of newspaper for your post—holiday meal snooze. Yes, now it's time to smile sweetly and **pop outta your pants** before spacing into a turkey high.

Best sleep ever.

AWESOME!

Singing the national anthem with a big crowd

Thanksgiving includes football.

Hey, don't look at me. They're not my rules. But hands up if you grew up in a house where the women **mashed potatoes** and set tables while the guys stood around a big screen holding beers. Yeah, if you celebrated Thanksgiving by watching **grown men** crack each other's skulls while running around chasing a ball, you are not alone.

And there is something beautiful about football games.

Especially if you go to one live.

See, when we walk into the stadium we're all strangers.

Pushing into opposite sides of the football field always feels like we're getting ready to battle, **getting ready to fight**, and getting ready to cheer. Grab your flag, pump your fist, and finish that beer as we all amp up for the big game.

And that's why it's a beautiful moment when the national anthem hits the speakers and slices through the crowd. Suddenly we all stop for a minute and swish and swirl together . . . standing beside each other, **singing the same song**, proud of our home country, and all just standing strong . . .

AWESOME!

The loudest guy at the game

....

There's always one.

It's the beer belly guy with the megaphone, the face-painted lady with the dangly earrings, or the boozy teens with the letters on their chests. These folks don't rest, and **we all can attest** that they make our entire fan experience better than the best.

The loudest guy at the game cheers on the crowd. The loudest guy at the game makes the home fans proud.

The loudest guy at the game . . . is just really damn loud.

AWESOME!

When your favorite football team is in the big nationally televised game

....

Maybe you're the San Diego Chargers fan who watches every game wearing a football helmet and a big foam thumb on your couch. Maybe you're a die-hard freak for the Redskins, Patriots, or Jets. Or maybe you can't stop watching the Cincinnati Bengals climb up the standings.

Whatever your bag, one thing's for sure: There's nothing finer than watching your favorite team on national television. For so many reasons:

- **Pressure.** The audience for your team shoots up exponentially and your favorite players are broadcast into strange living rooms around the country. This is the big moment where everybody will judge you, so you better be ready to perform. Don't let it get to your head.

- **Better announcers.** Okay, you may lose some of the local favorites who cheer for your club all the time. But you gain the veterans who've been broadcasting for years. Plus, don't forget the better 3D graphics and special blimp camera.

- **Feel like you're home.** Hey, if you don't live in your hometown anymore, the big show might be one of the few chances you get to see your team play. How great is it to watch your across-the-country team in your new local bar? That's what I'm talking about.

Yes, when your favorite football team is in the nationally televised game, it feels special sitting down at home and watching them play on the big stage. So take the phone off the hook, **make some popcorn**, and settle in for a great night with a few million friends.

AWESOME!

The Echo Meal

....

The Echo Meal is any perfectly re-created plate of turkey, veggies, stuffing, and pie made from all the leftovers from yesterday's pig-out. Microwaved brussels sprouts, steamed turkey chunks, and stirred up gravy all combine into a perfect follow-up to the feast.

AWESOME!

Getting through it

....

T hat was a tough one.

Come on in and stop for a second to shake your head, **dust yourself off**, and look back at how far you've come.

Sure, it's been a long year. Some crushing lows slapped you and smacked you around. There were times your heart dipped and you squinted back tears while your stomach squeezed so tightly you couldn't sleep. There were moments you walked around in a **glossy-eyeball daze**—when loved ones hurt, friends didn't stay, or someone dear to your heart slowly drifted away.

Sleepless nights, stressful nights, with teething babies, slurring customers, **bad bosses**, bickering boyfriends, or blank computer screens. You were feeling and you were dealing and you were reeling and you were healing.

But as you walked your hard path down your long and bumpy road, some little **drops of confidence** dripped like coffee into your head and into your heart. As you stumbled and got back up, a **quiet inner strength** slowly seeped into your bones. And as you climbed over obstacles set in your way, some relaxed satisfaction and growing self-awareness glimmered like bright lights at the bottom of your stomach.

Yes, this year changed you and grew you in so many ways

you don't even feel or notice yet. As you struggled you empathized, as you slipped you understood, as you worked you earned . . .

. . . as you looked you learned

. . . as you dared you grew

. . . and as you jumped you flew.

Your dreams are still focusing and your passion is growing. Your energy is still bubbling and your story keeps going.

You've been through so much and gained **a year's supply** of experience along the way. You're stronger than you were last year and stronger than you realize. Sure, there were times you bent, but you definitely didn't break. There were times you caved, but you definitely didn't flake.

Listen up: You got bigger, you got better, and you got the scars to prove it.

So stop for a second today to smile and look back at everything you've done this year . . . everything you've seen . . . everywhere you've been . . .

You've taken more illegal naps and had more blurry-eyed late nights.

You've danced to more wedding songs and smiled at more beautiful sights.

You've seen more scorching sunsets and heard more head-bopping songs.

You've tripped a few times, but, baby, you kept rolling right along.

Yes, you've hugged more old friends and kissed some brand-new pretty faces.

You've cheered more on the sidelines and visited some brand-new pretty places.

You tasted more meals, you got more deals, and you've sniffed more flower blossoms.

And you made it all the way through this year because you're so completely

AWESOME!

ABOUT THE AUTHOR

Neil Pasricha is terrible at wrapping gifts, can't carve a turkey, and always forgets birthdays. He's just a regular guy who loves seeing the first shipment of eggnog in the store, eating all the chocolate in the Advent calendar at once, and driving around town to see all the Christmas lights.

My Awesome Things

_____

_____

_____

_____

_____

_____

_____

_____

_____

_____

AWESOME!

WHAT'S YOUR AWESOME THING

Let's keep the awesome going! If you'd like your awesome thing to be considered for use on www.1000awesomethings.com, just write up something less than five hundred words and send it over. We'll pick some favorites and mail those selected a basket of awesome goodies for your troubles. Go to the website to see how to submit. Thanks for reading, thanks for sending your thoughts, and thanks for being

AWESOME!

OTHER BOOKS IN THE AWESOME SERIES BY *NEW YORK TIMES* BESTSELLING AUTHOR NEIL PASRICHA

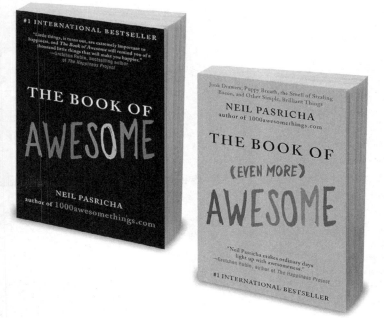

"Laugh-out-loud funny." — Wired.com

"Strangely heartwarming...perfect for rainy days."
— *The New Yorker*

T345-0813